Mandolin Picking Tunes

CELTIC GEMS

by Tommy Norris

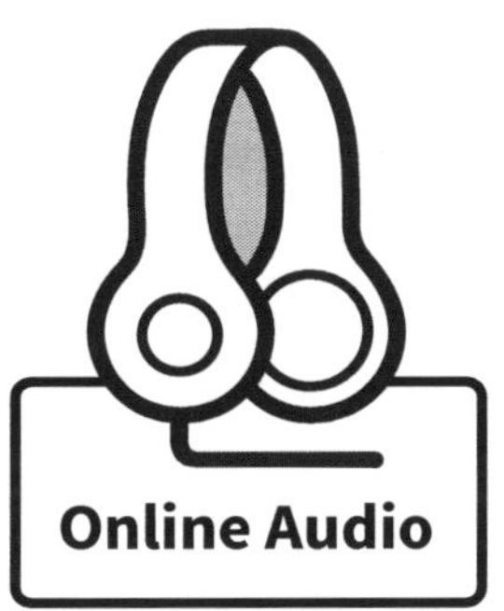

To access the online audio go to:

WWW.MELBAY.COM/30920MEB

The Prucha PREMIUM - Varnish lacquer mandolin cover image courtesy of Prucha Bluegrass instruments.

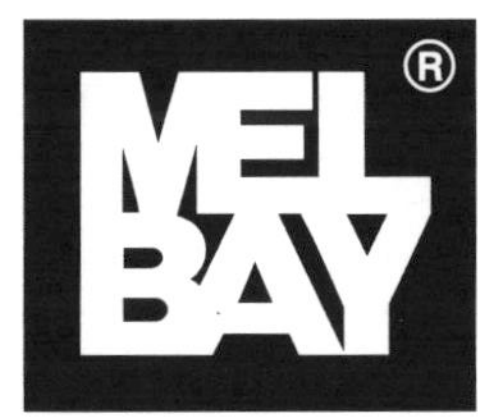

WWW.MELBAY.COM

Preface

This collection of 30 traditional to modern *Celtic Gems* is arranged half and half as either simple single-line melodies with suggested accompaniment chords, or as more challenging but fulfilling intermediate melody/chord solos capable of standing on their own.

From "Carolan's Dream" and "Cooley's Reel" to the anonymous "Londonderry Air" (later known as "Danny Boy") and William Bay's modern "The Highlander," these settings offer engaging melodies that have stood the test of time.

All of the tunes are shown in both standard notation and tablature in mandolin and guitar-friendly keys. After listening to the online audio examples as played by the author, you'll ultimately want to add your own interpretive signature to these lively reels and jigs and tender ballads.

We hope you'll find several melodies herein to share with friends at musical gatherings or add to your solo Celtic repertoire.

Index of Tunes

An Dro

Rhythmically ♩ = 130

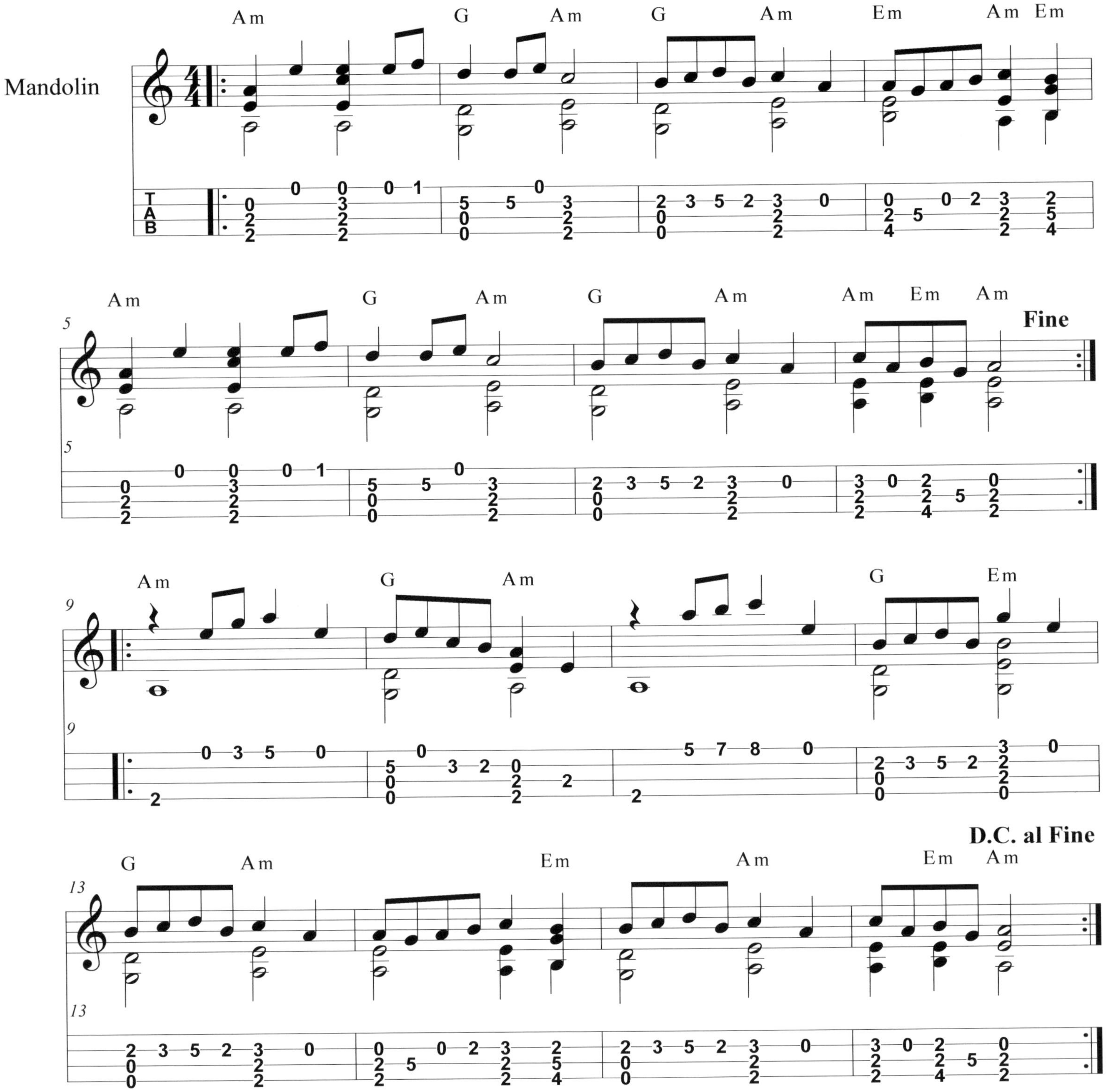

Mandolin

Am G Am G Am Em Am Em

Am G Am G Am Am Em Am **Fine**

Am G Am G Em

D.C. al Fine

G Am Em Am Em Am

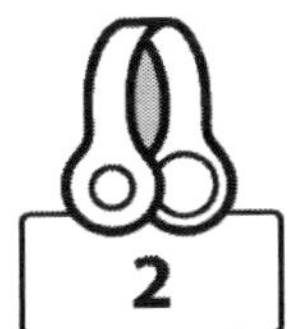

Chanter's Tune

Moderato 𝅗𝅥 = 88

A

Mandolin

A5 G A5 G A G D Em Bm

A5 G A5 G A G A5 Em A5 Em A5

1. **Fine** 2.

B

A Em D A G A G Em D Em Bm

A5 Em A G A5 Em A5 A5 Em A5

1. 2. **D.C. al Fine**

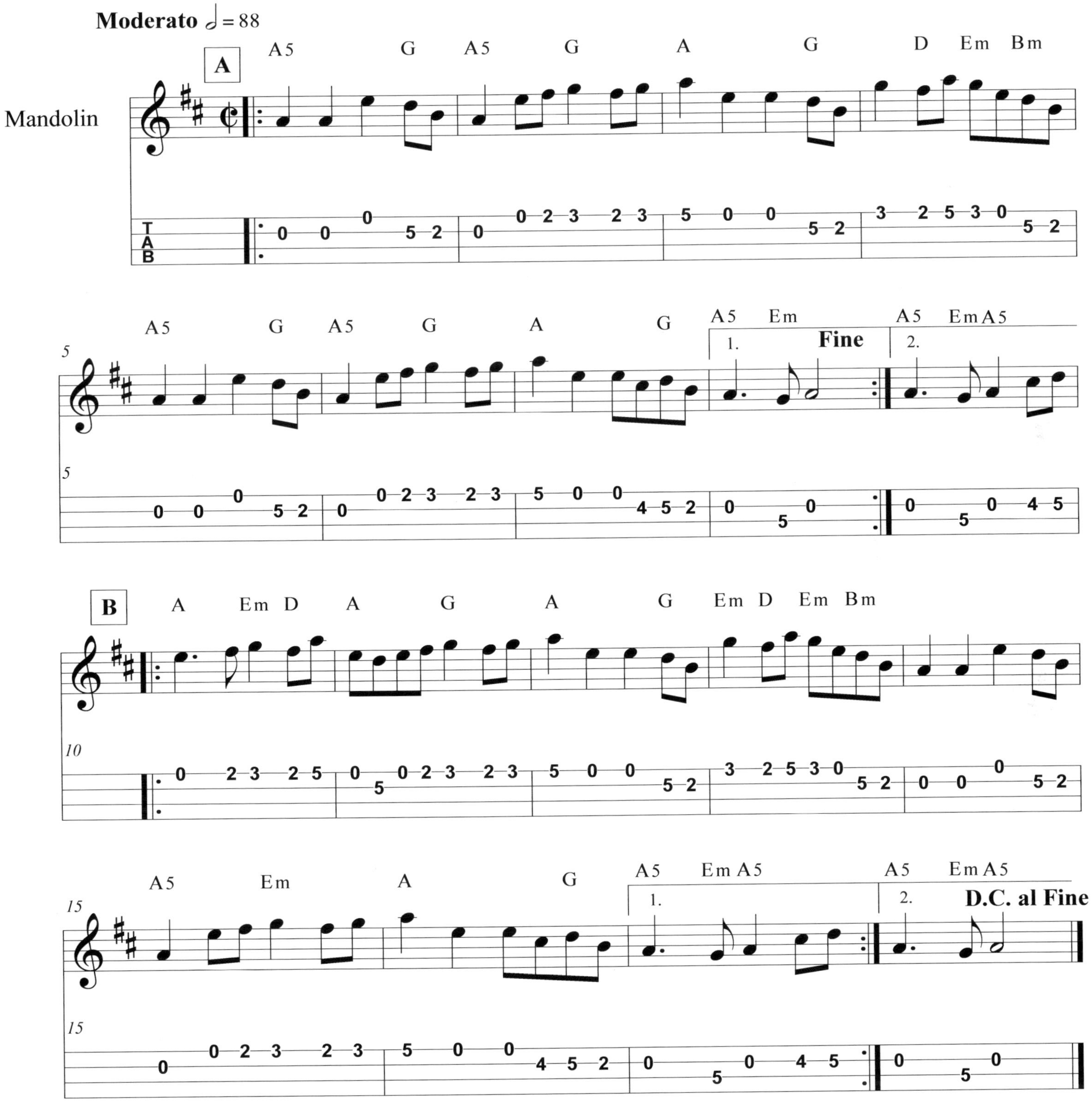

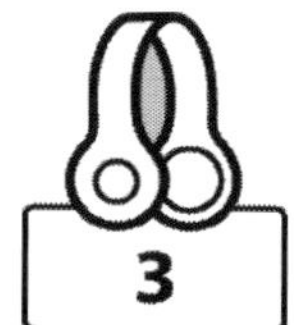

Carolan's Dream

Gently ♩ = 76

Turlough O'Carolan

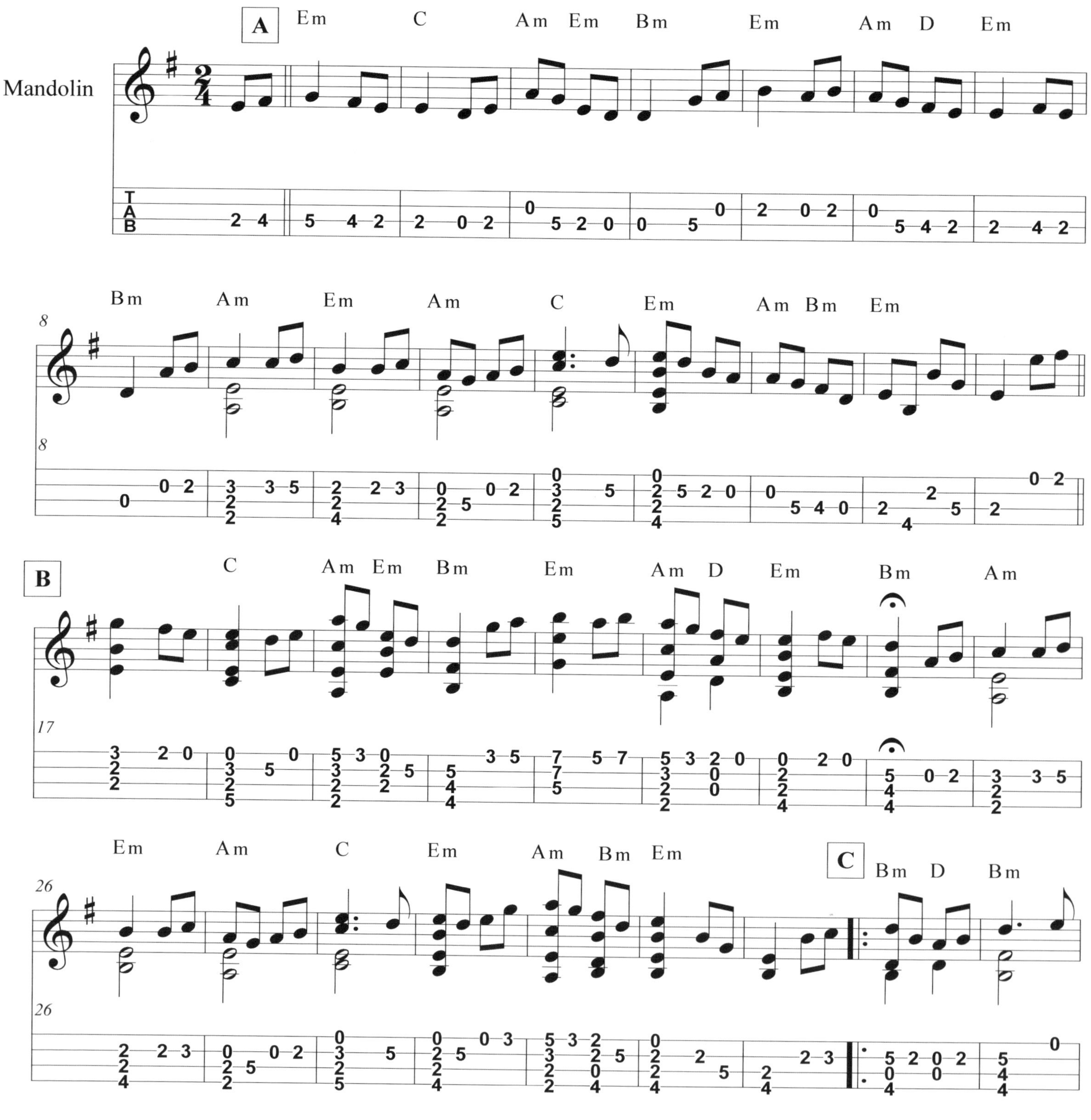

Mandolin

A

Em C Am Em Bm Em Am D Em

Bm Am Em Am C Em Am Bm Em

B

C Am Em Bm Em Am D Em Bm Am

Em Am C Em Am Bm Em

C

Bm D Bm

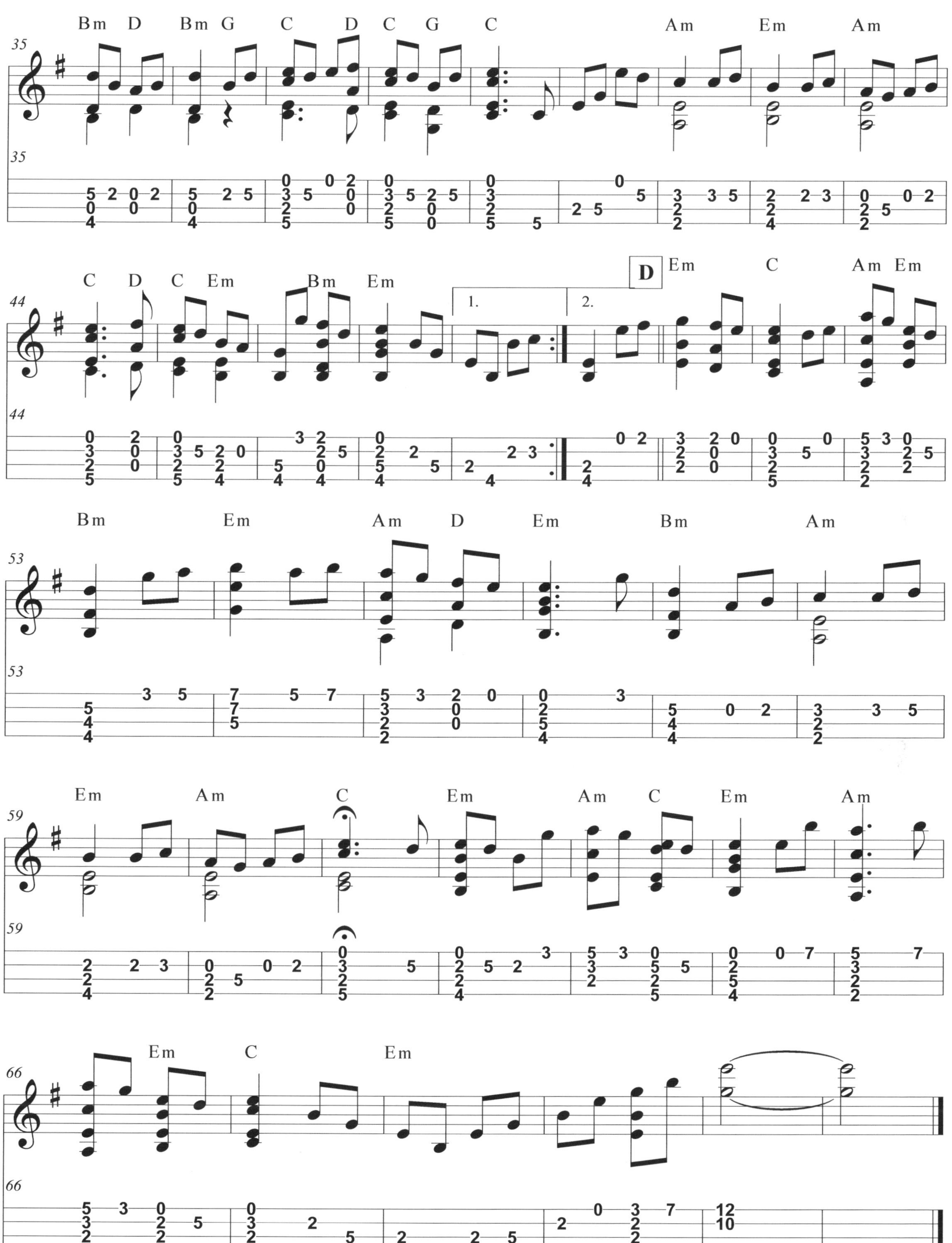
Bm D Bm G C D C G C Am Em Am
C D C Em Bm Em
1.
2.
D
Em C Am Em
Bm Em Am D Em Bm Am
Em Am C Em Am C Em Am
Em C Em

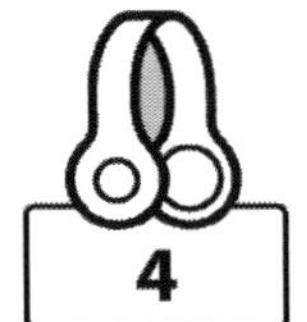

Clancy's Wake

Inspired by the Celtic classic slip jig "The Butterfly".

Slip Jig Tempo ♩. = 100

William Bay

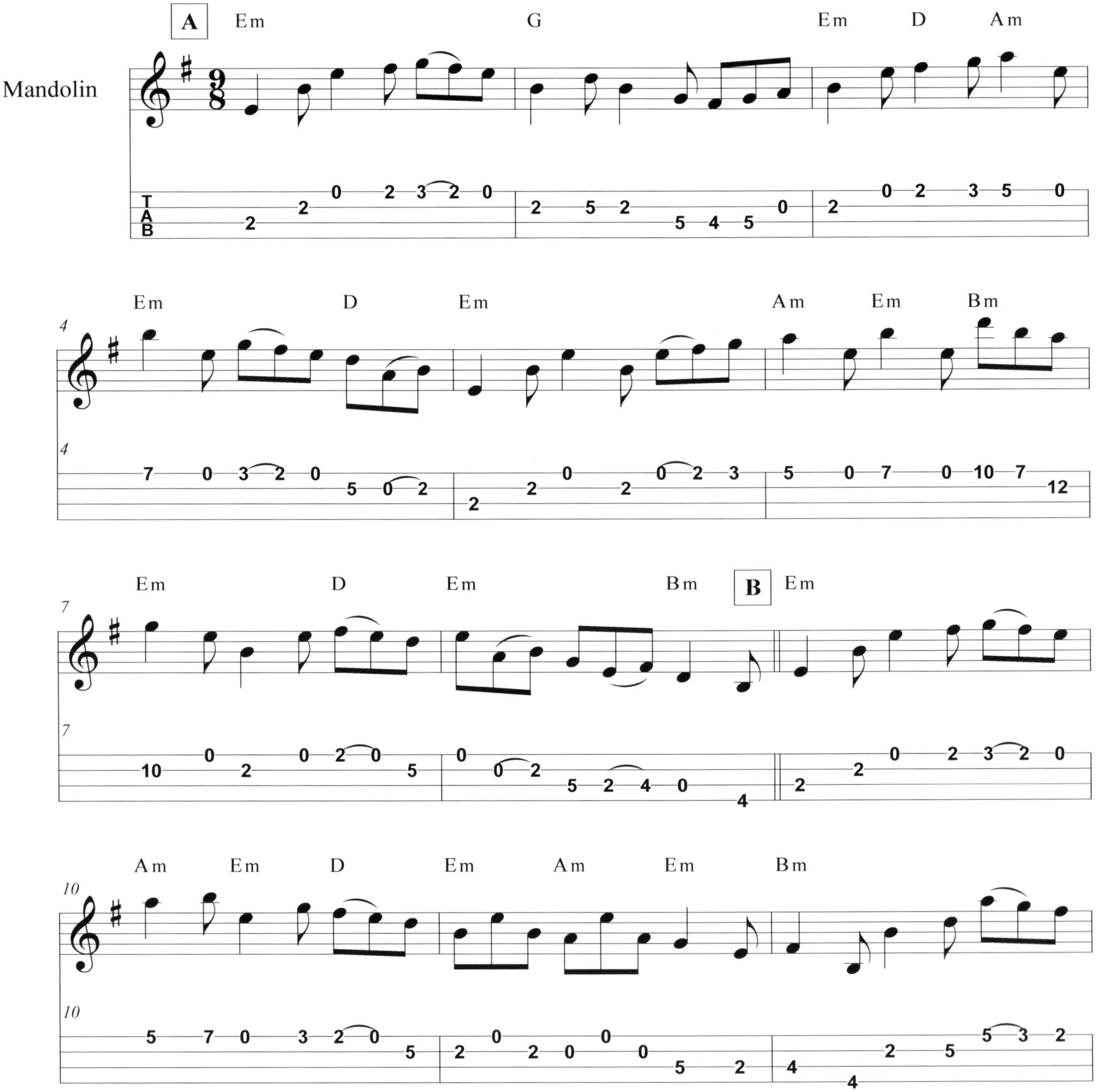

A

Em G Em D Am

Mandolin

4

Em D Em Am Em Bm

7

Em D Em Bm

B

Em

10

Am Em D Em Am Em Bm

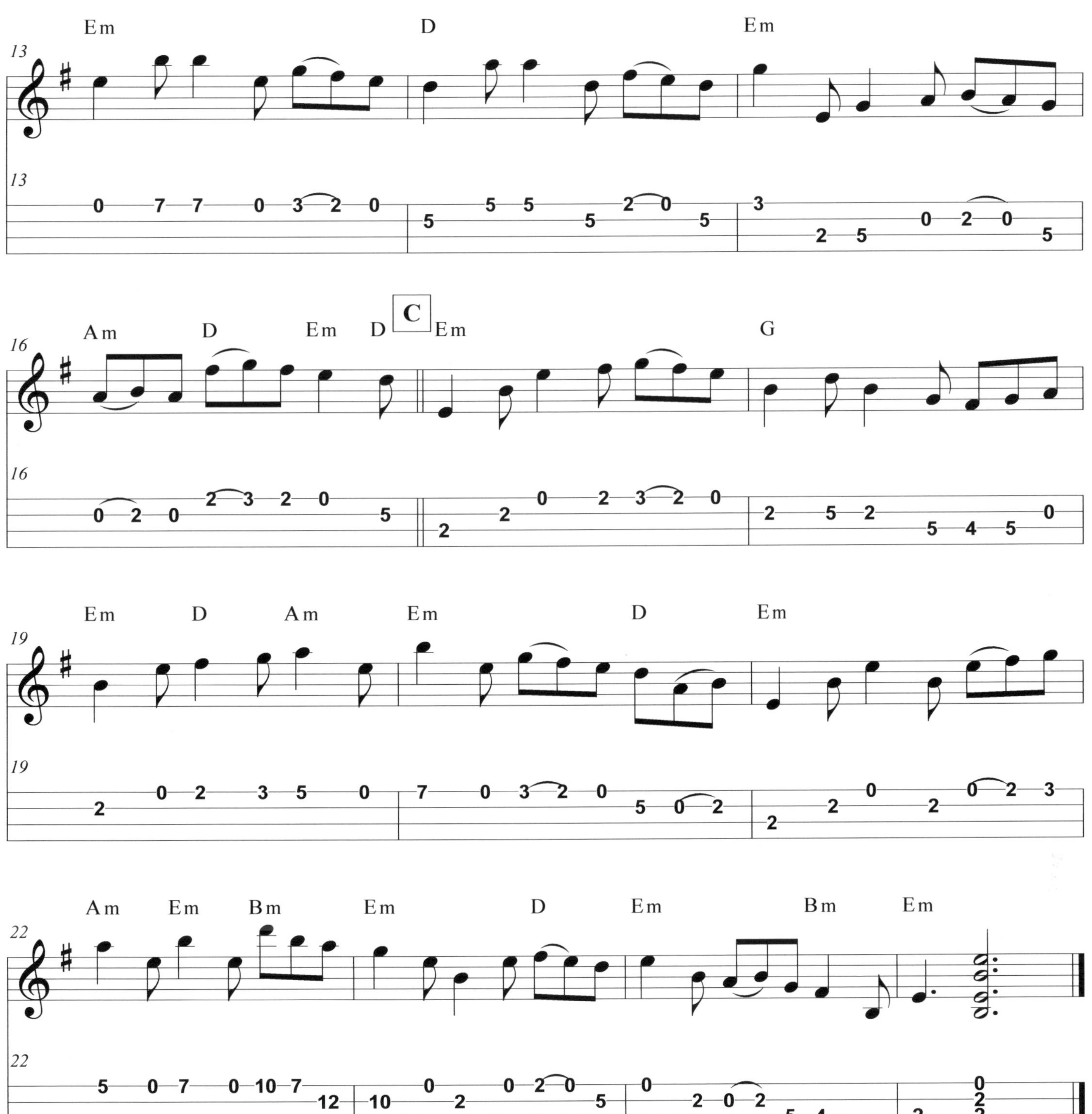
13
Em
D
Em
16
Am
D
Em
D
C
Em
G
19
Em
D
Am
Em
D
Em
22
Am
Em
Bm
Em
D
Em
Bm
Em

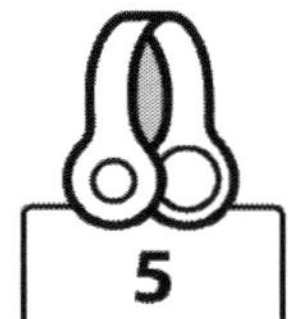

Cooley's Reel

Rhythmically ♩ = 138

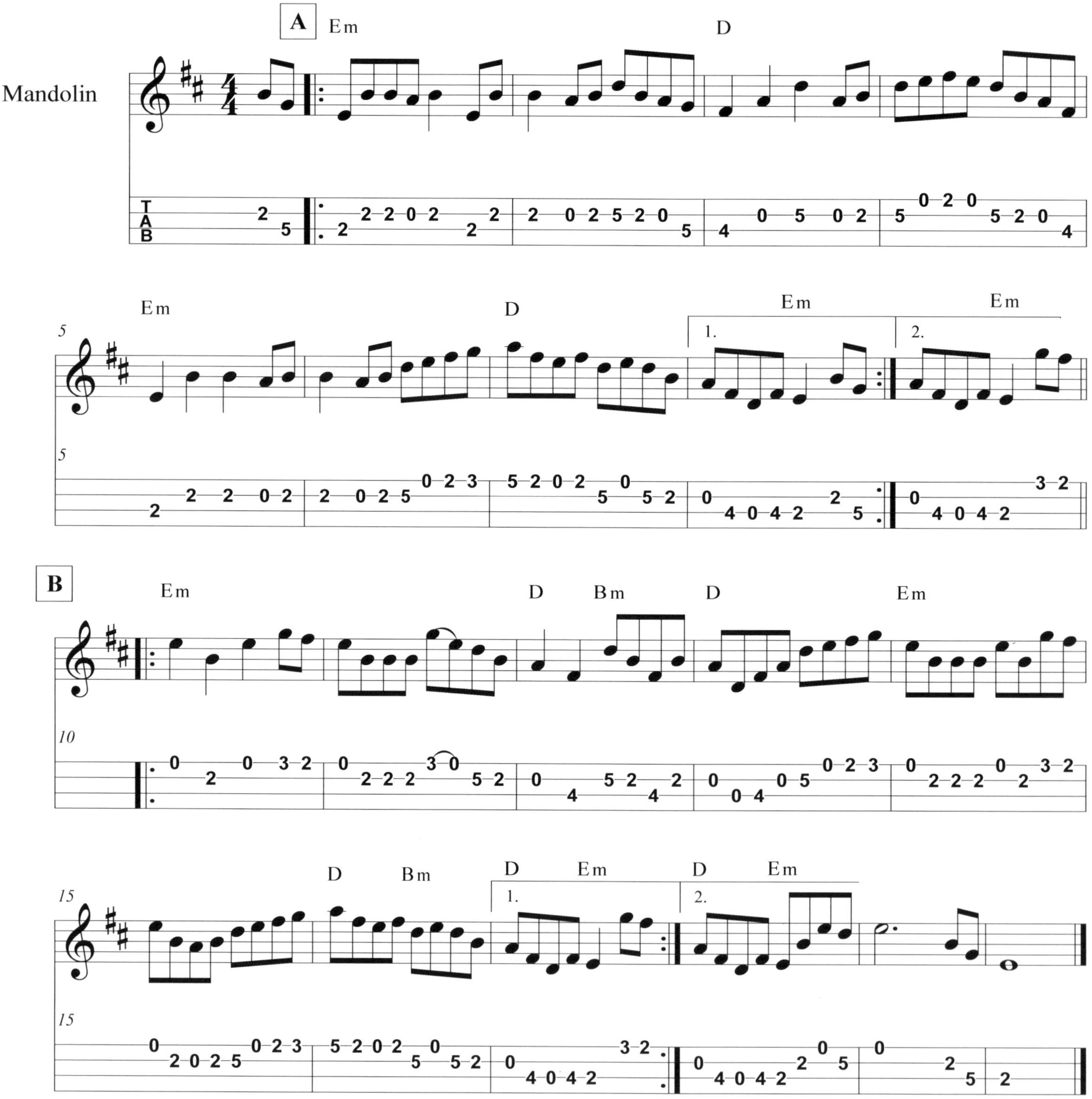

A

Mandolin

Em D

Em D Em Em

B

Em D Bm D Em

D Bm D Em D Em

Courting Is a Pleasure

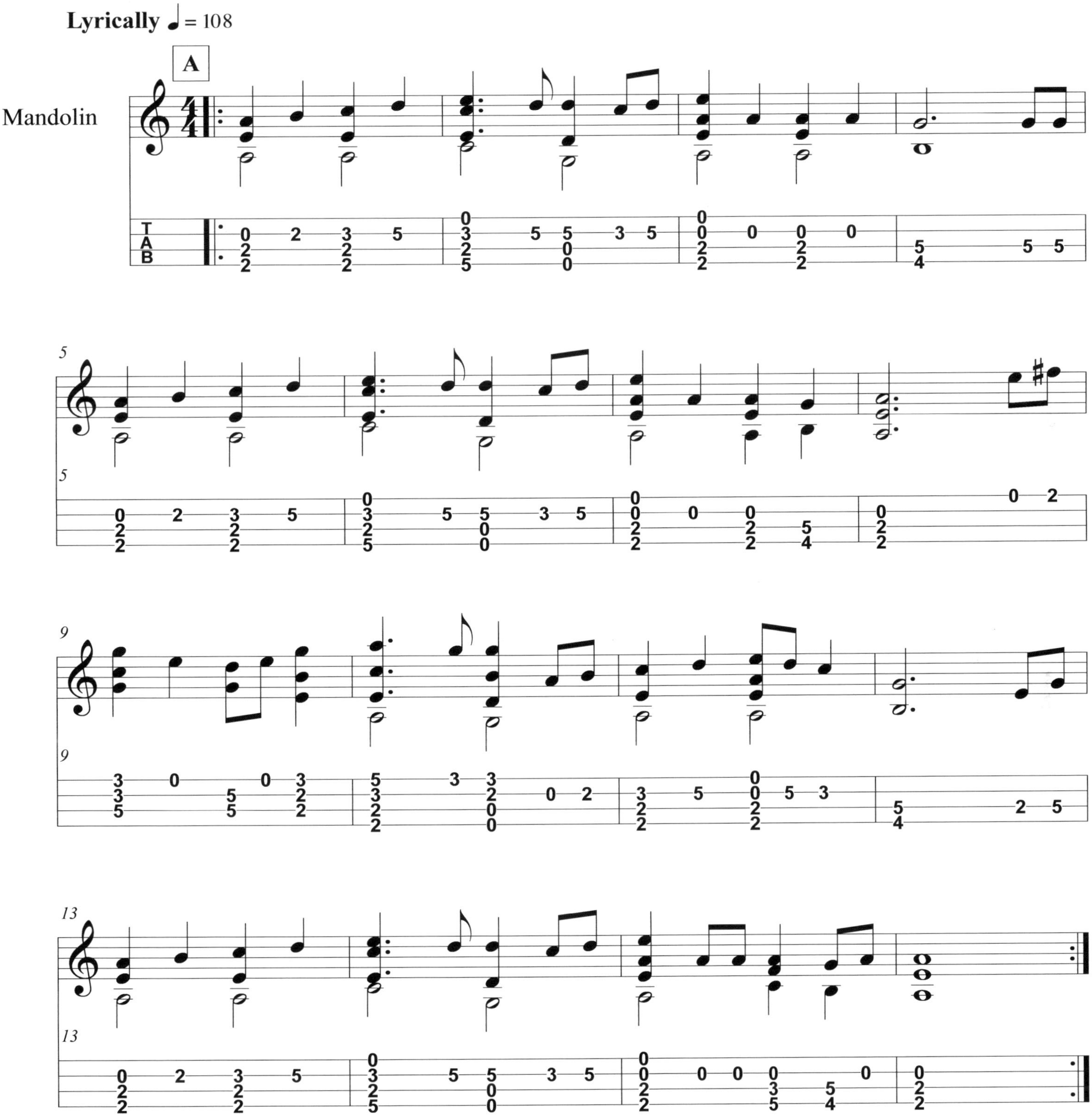

Lyrically ♩ = 108

A

Mandolin

The Mist-Covered Mountain

Jig

Moderate Tempo ♩. = 100

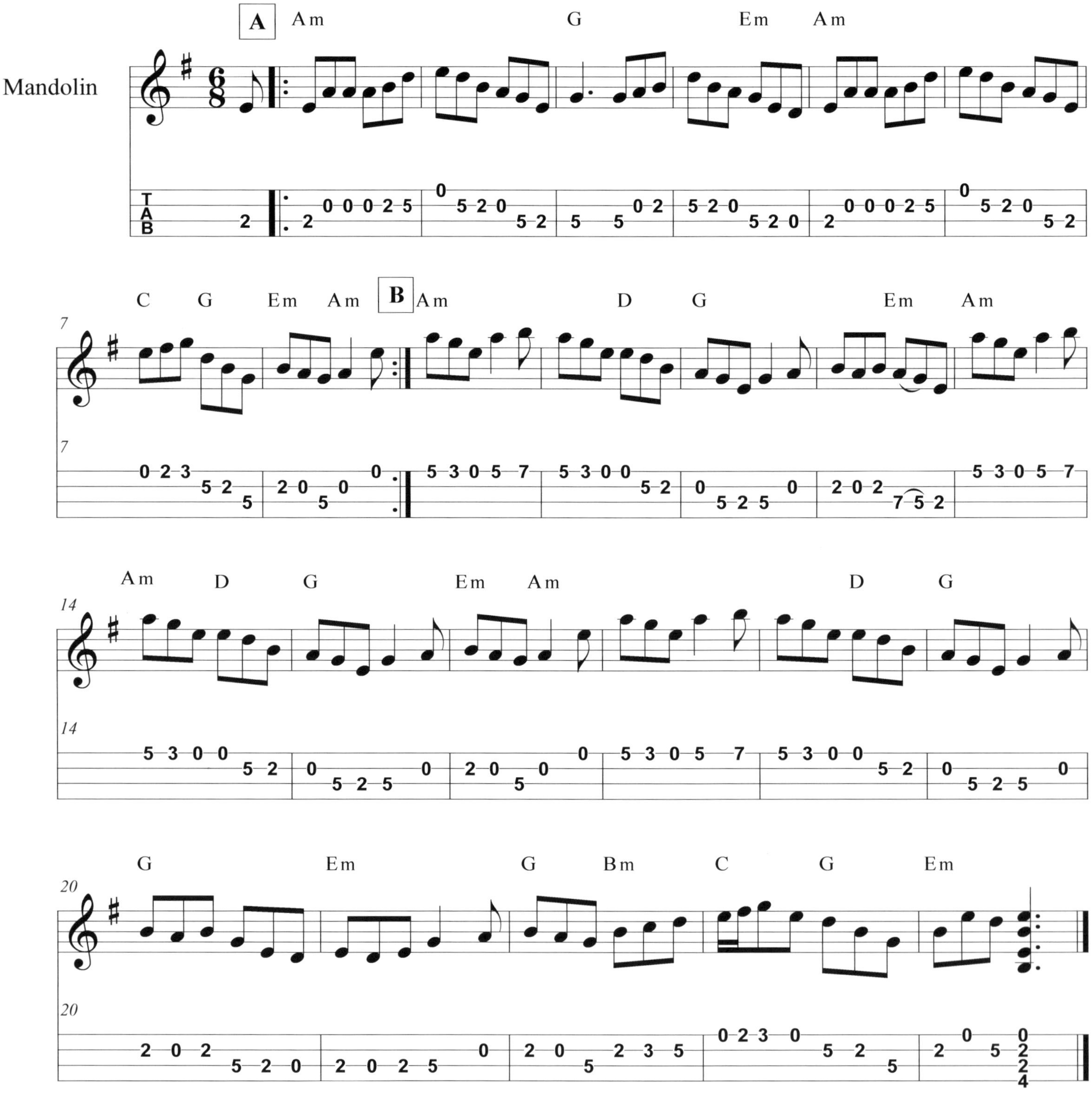

Mandolin

A: Am G Em Am

C G Em Am | B: Am D G Em Am

Am D G Em Am D G

G Em G Bm C G Em

Guilderoy

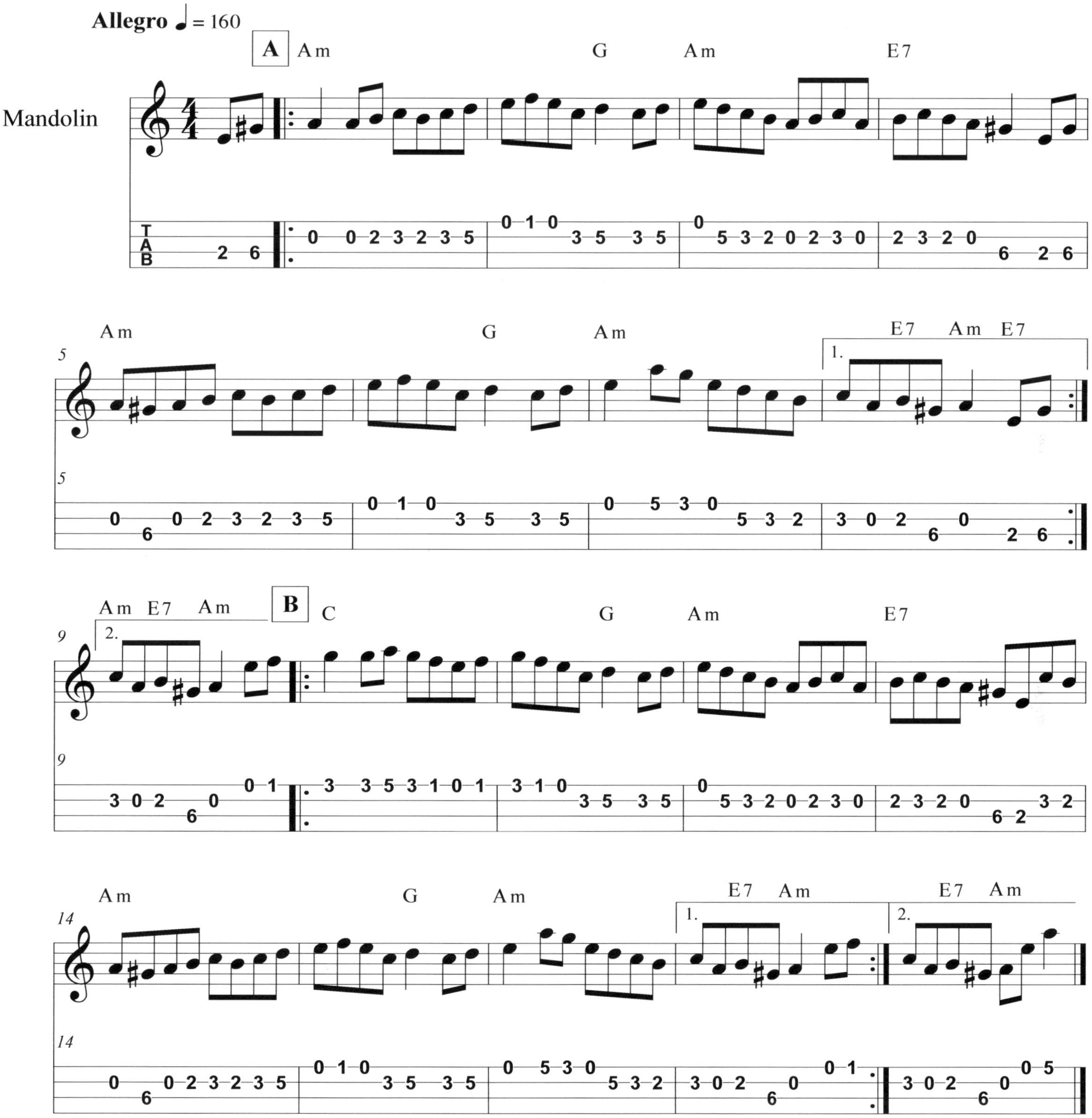

Allegro ♩ = 160

Mandolin

A — Am | G Am | E7

T A B: 2 6 | 0 0 2 3 2 3 5 | 0 1 0 3 5 3 5 | 0 5 3 2 0 2 3 0 | 2 3 2 0 6 2 6

5 — Am | G Am | 1. E7 Am E7

0 6 0 2 3 2 3 5 | 0 1 0 3 5 3 5 | 0 5 3 0 5 3 2 | 3 0 2 6 0 2 6

9 — 2. Am E7 Am | B — C | G Am | E7

3 0 2 6 0 0 1 | 3 3 5 3 1 0 1 | 3 1 0 3 5 3 5 | 0 5 3 2 0 2 3 0 | 2 3 2 0 6 2 3 2

14 — Am | G Am | 1. E7 Am | 2. E7 Am

0 6 0 2 3 2 3 5 | 0 1 0 3 5 3 5 | 0 5 3 0 5 3 2 | 3 0 2 6 0 0 1 | 3 0 2 6 0 0 5

Greyfriars Bobby

William Bay

Tenderly ♩ = 92

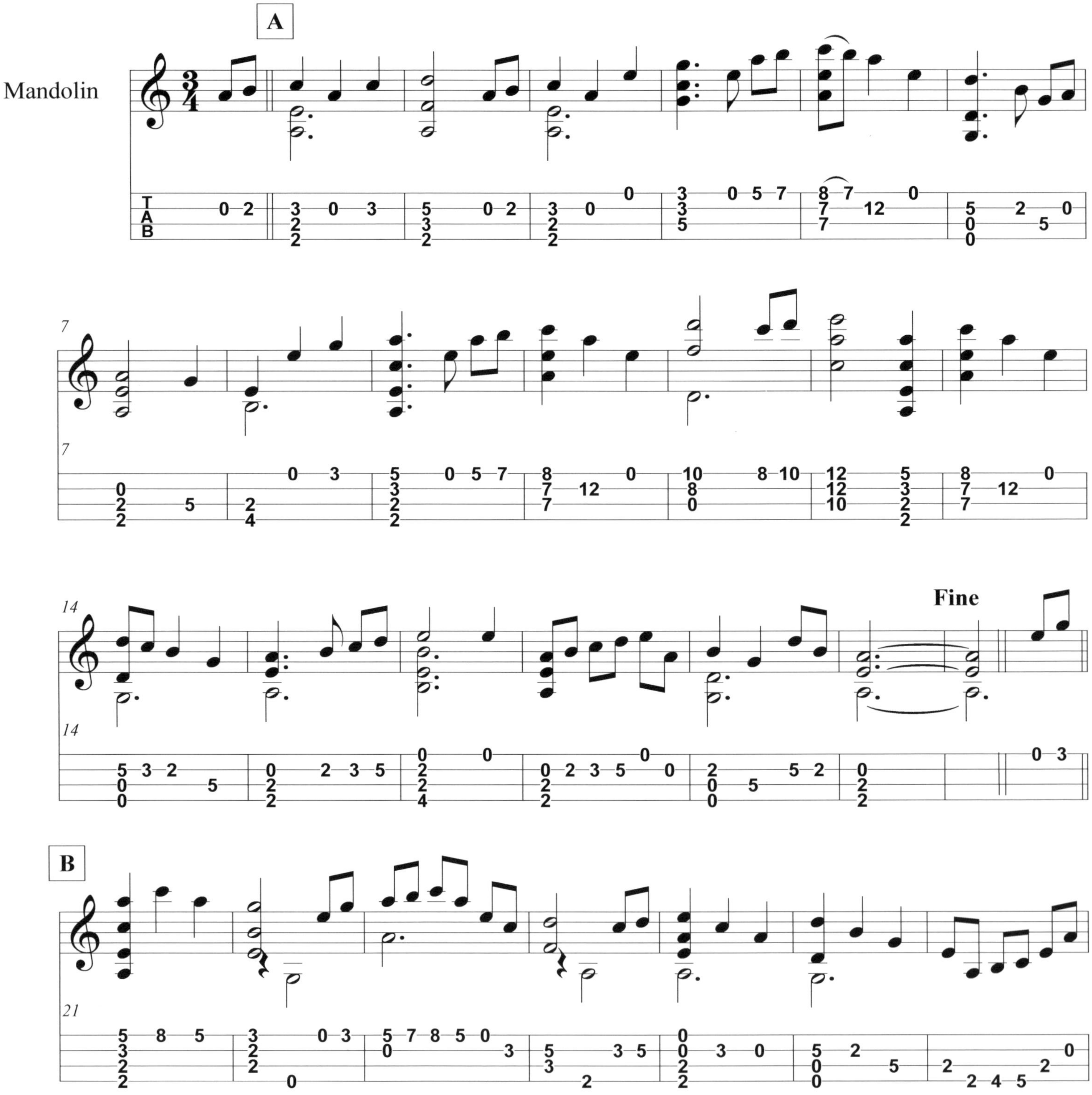

A

Mandolin

Fine

B

28
28
3 5 0 5 7 8 12 7 7 10 8 7 5 0 8 10 3 0 3 7 5 5 3 2 2

D.C. al Fine

32
32
2 0 0 5 2 5 0 2 2 0 3 0 5 0 0 3 2 0 5 2 2 2 0 2 3 5 0 2 0 2

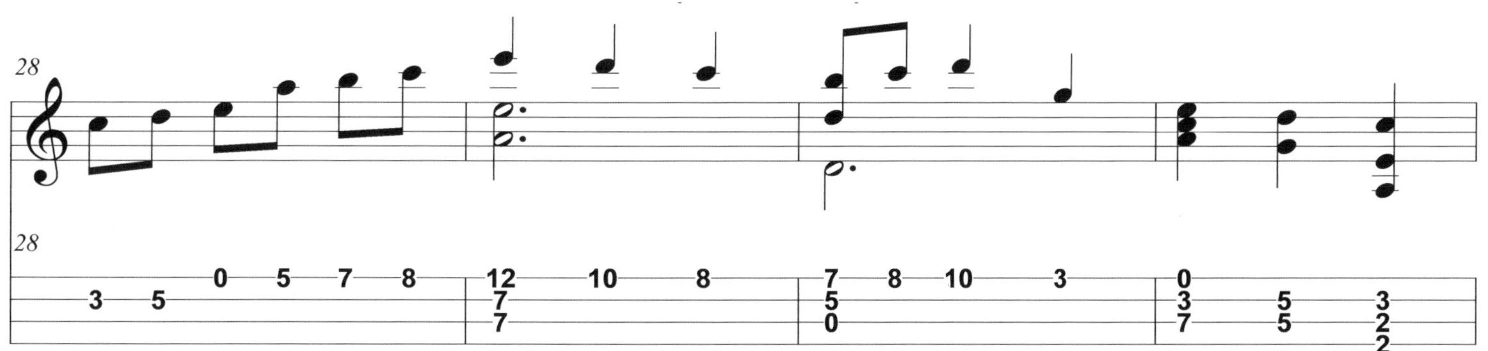

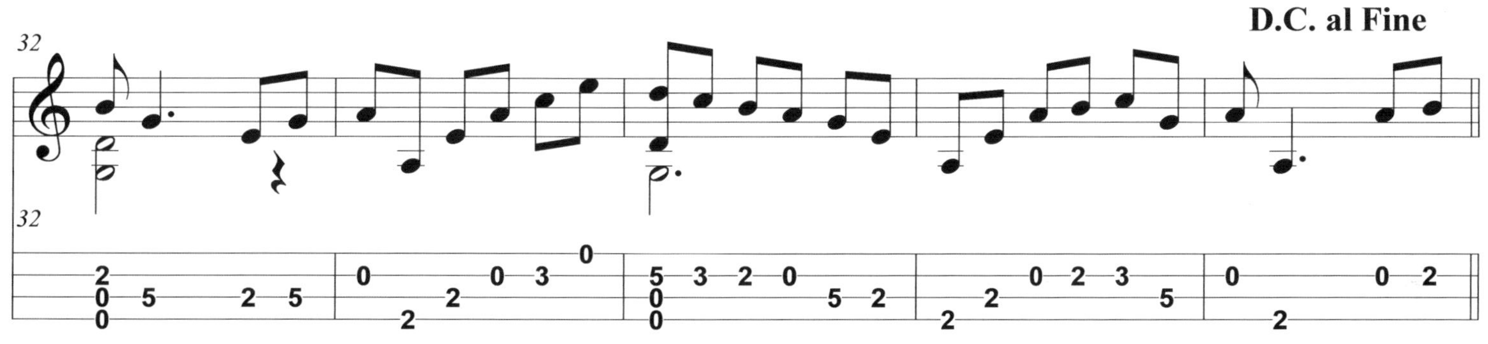

Hills of Ireland

Moderately ♩. = 112

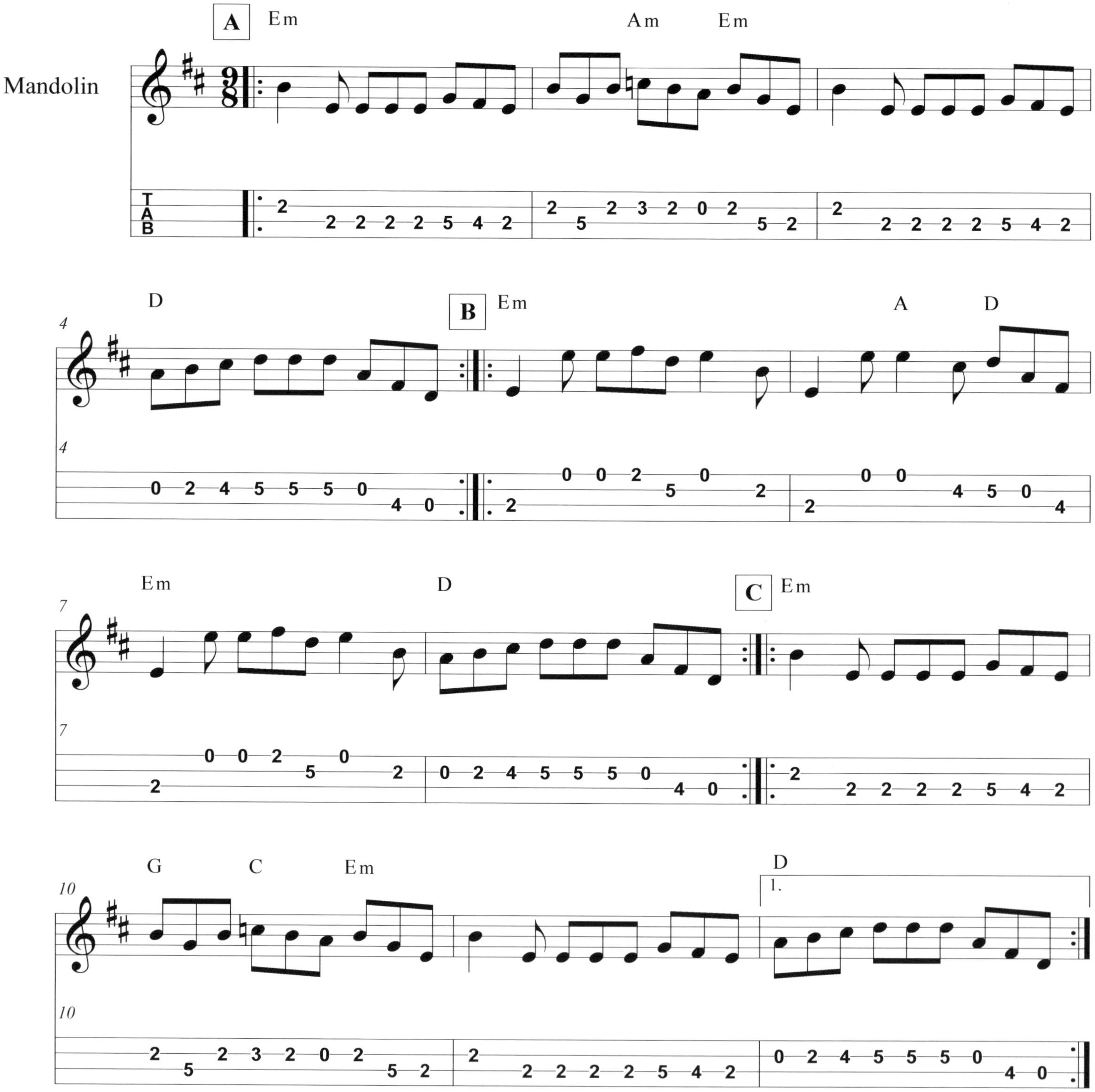

Mandolin

A — Em | Am Em | Em | D

B — Em | A D | Em | D

C — Em | G C Em | Em | 1. D

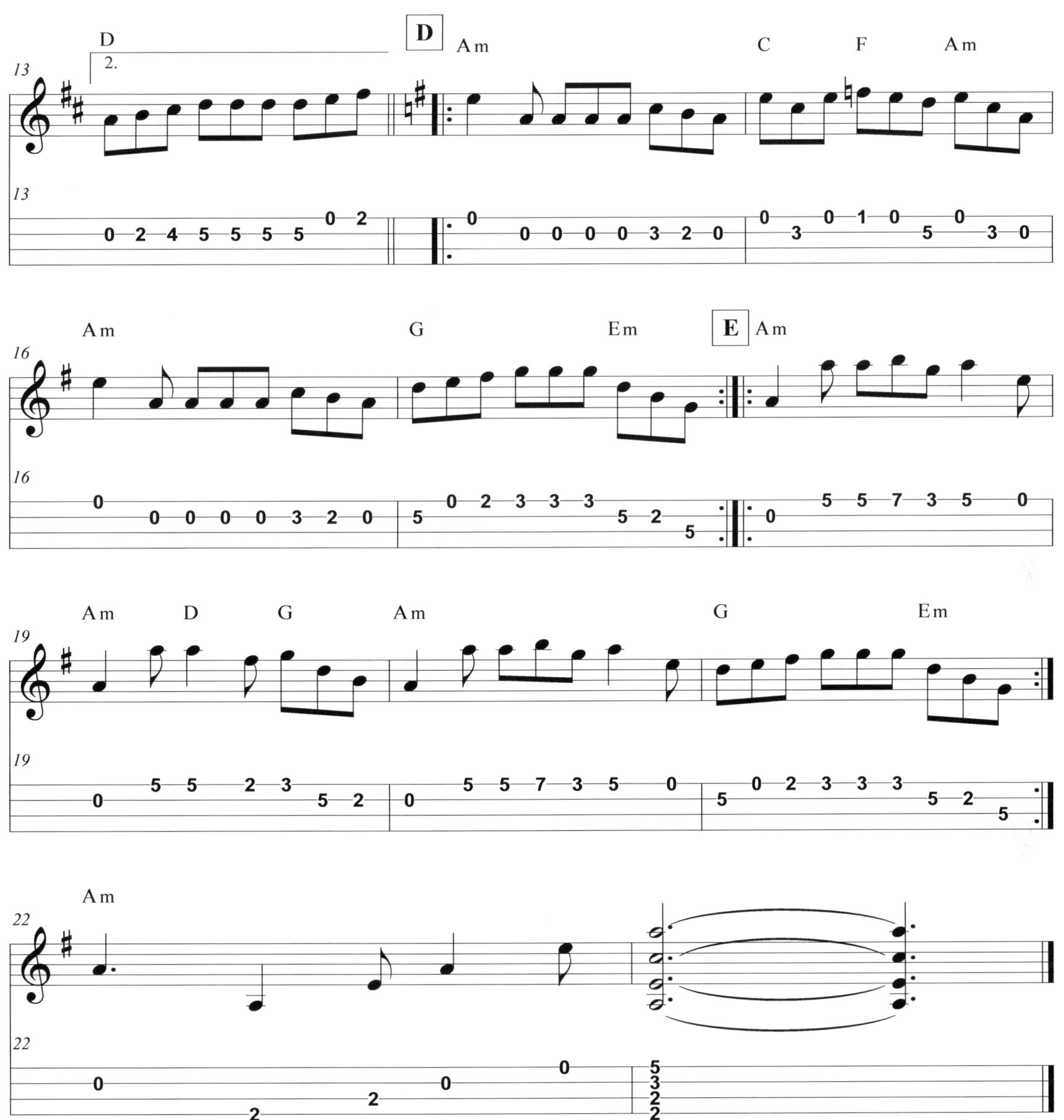
D
2.
D
Am
C
F
Am
Am
G
Em
E
Am
Am
D
G
Am
G
Em
Am

Londonderry Air

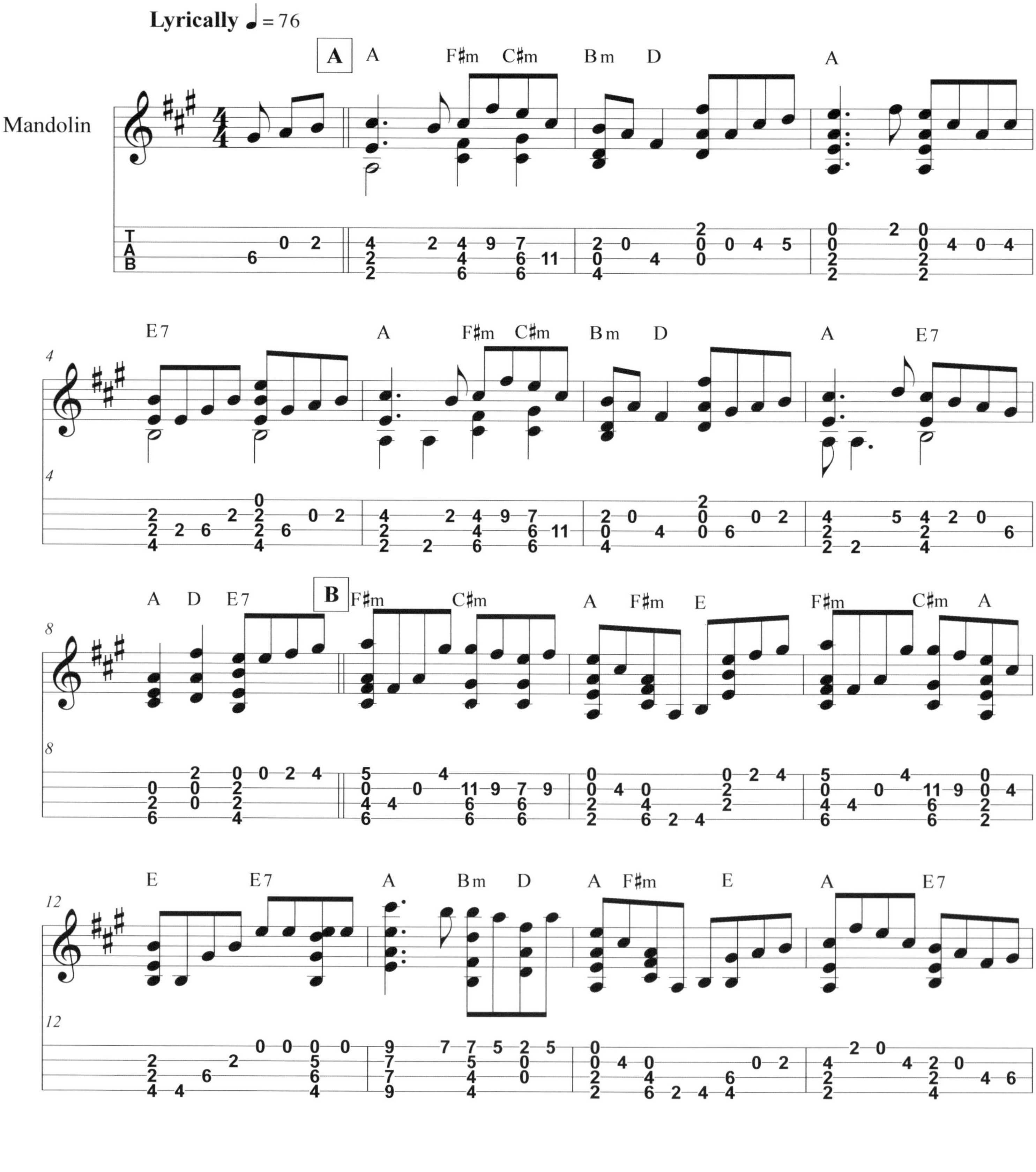

Lyrically ♩ = 76

Mandolin

A

A F♯m C♯m Bm D A

E7 A F♯m C♯m Bm D A E7

A D E7 **B** F♯m C♯m A F♯m E F♯m C♯m A

E E7 A Bm D A F♯m E A E7

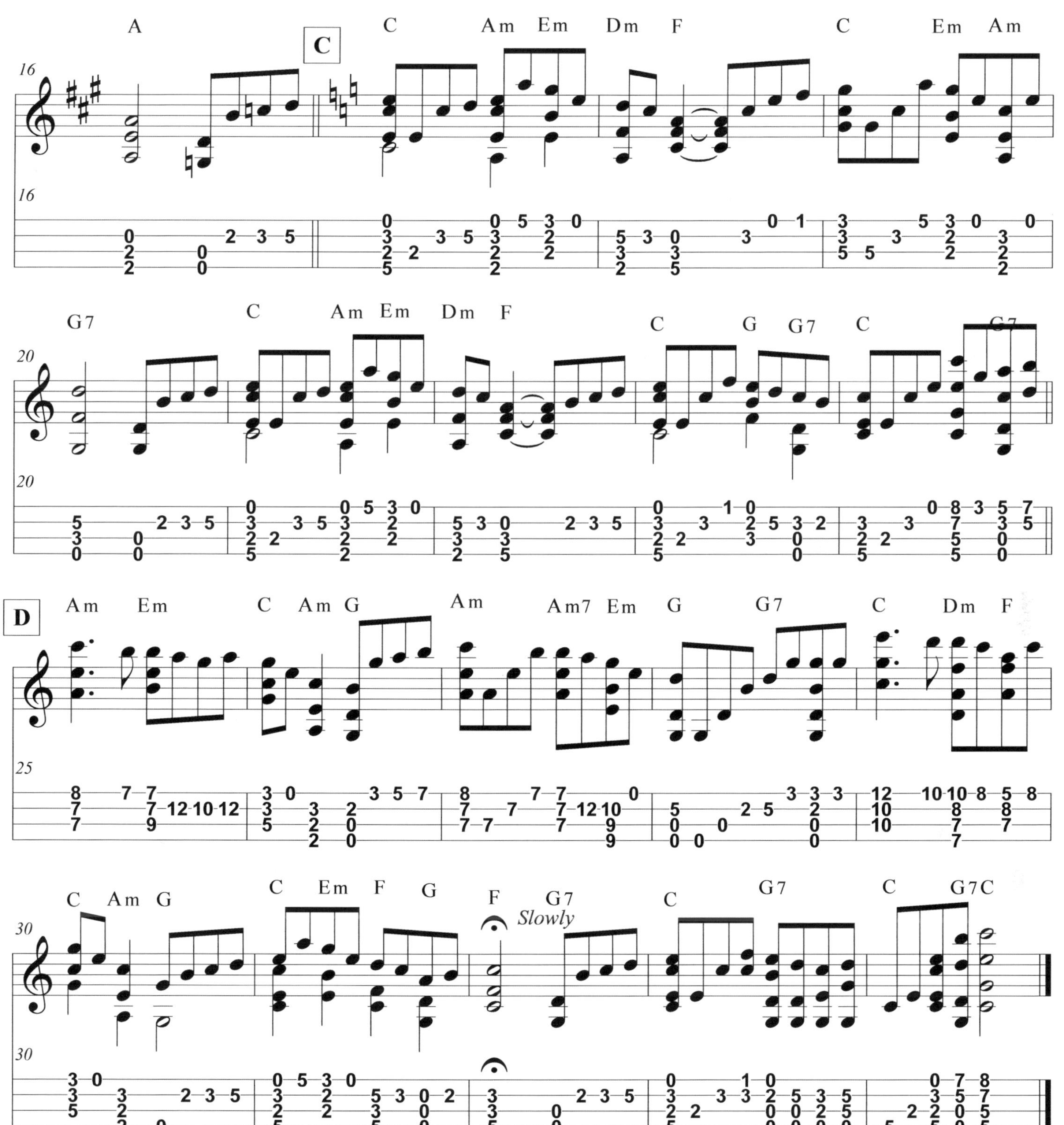
A
C
C Am Em Dm F C Em Am
G7 C Am Em Dm F C G G7 C G7
D
Am Em C Am G Am Am7 Em G G7 C Dm F
C Am G C Em F G F G7 C G7 C G7 C
Slowly

MacDonald, Lord of the Isles

Very Slow and Free ♩ = 68

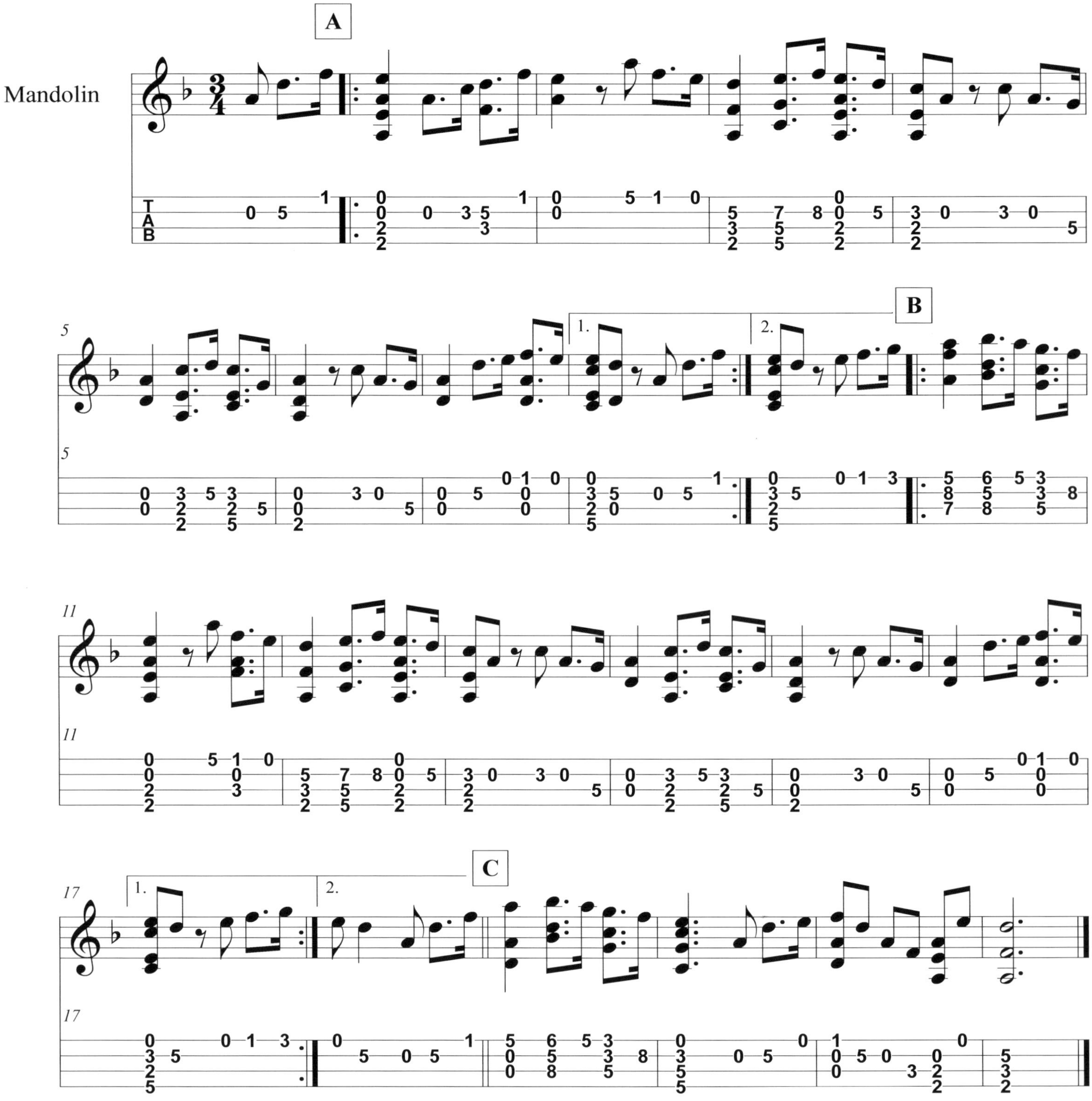

A

Mandolin

B

C

MacPherson's Farewell

13

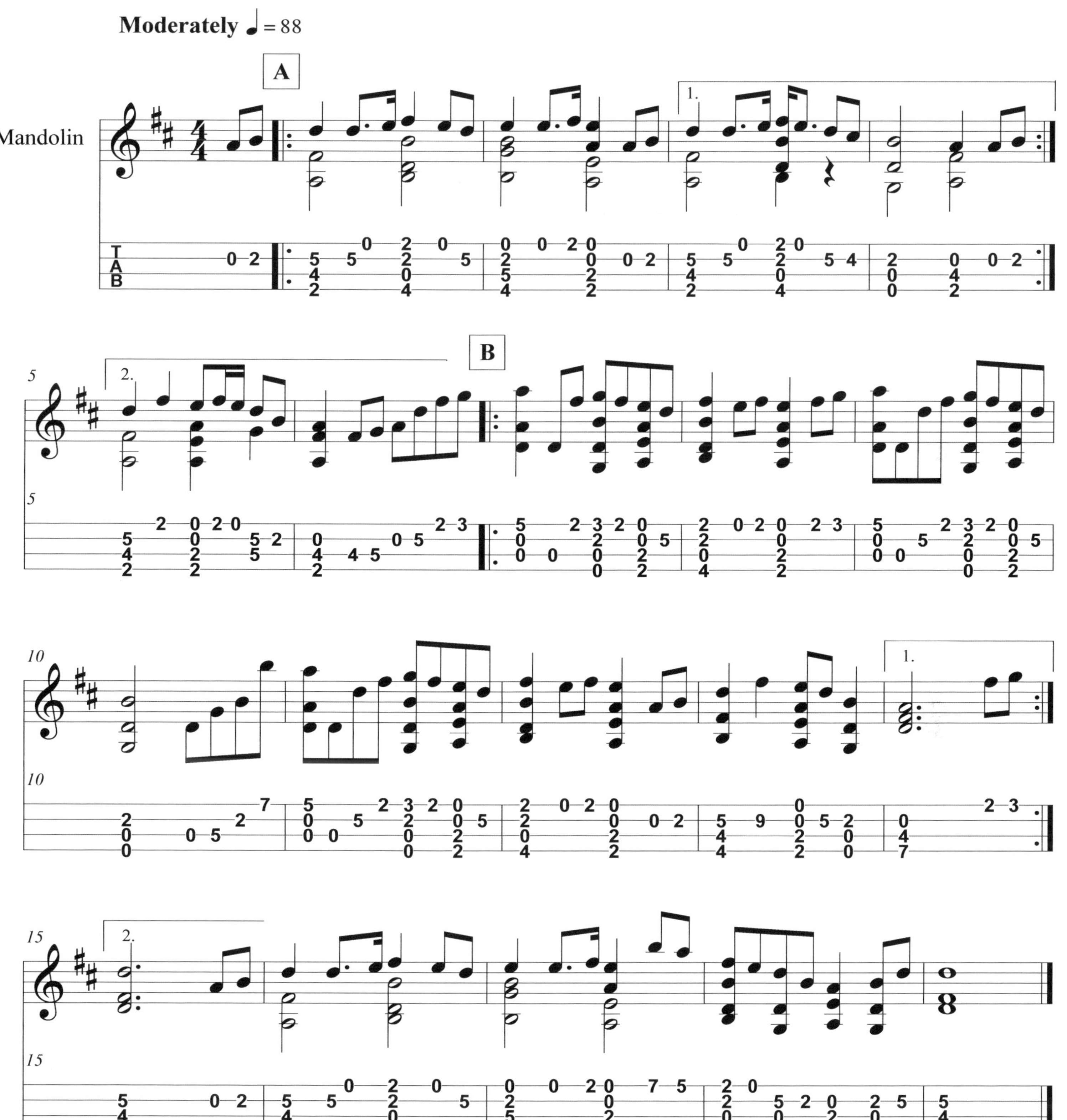

Ned of the Hill

Lyrically ♩ = 96

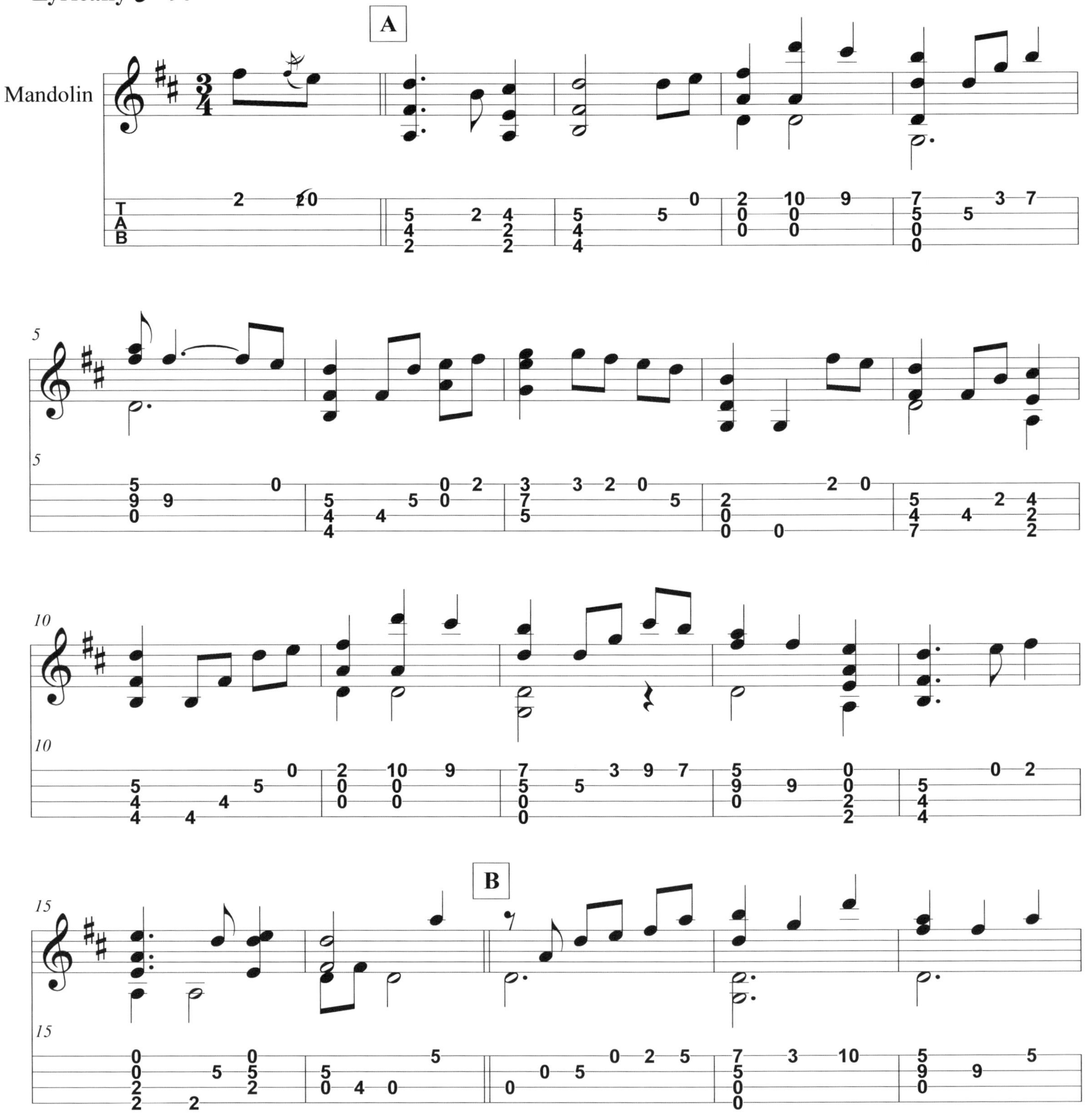

A

Mandolin

B

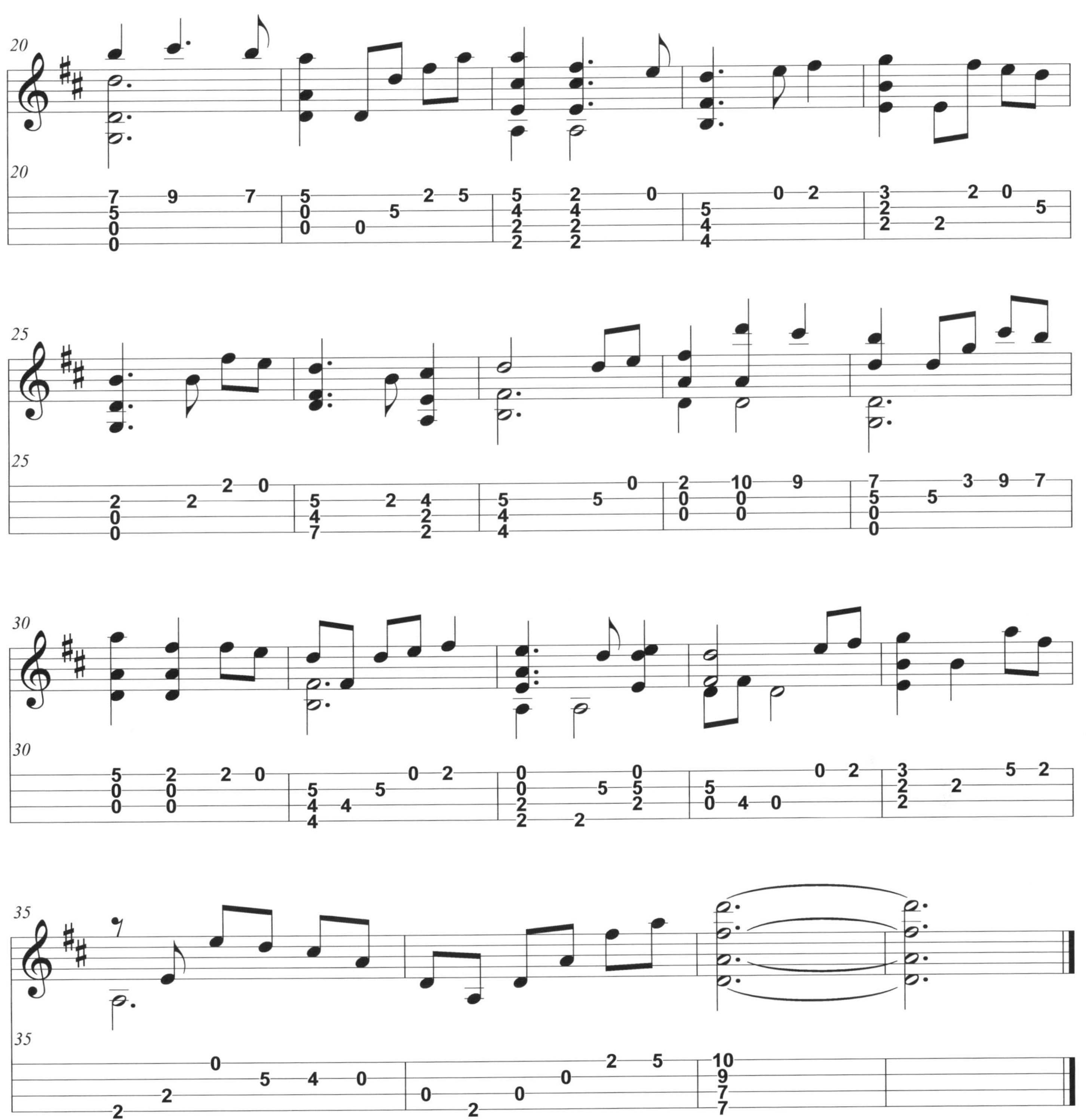

My Spirited Love

Spirited ♩ = 125

A

Mandolin

D G D A D G D A G D

D G D A D G D A7sus D **Fine**

B

D A7sus G D A7sus A7

D A7sus D G D A G D **D.C. al Fine**

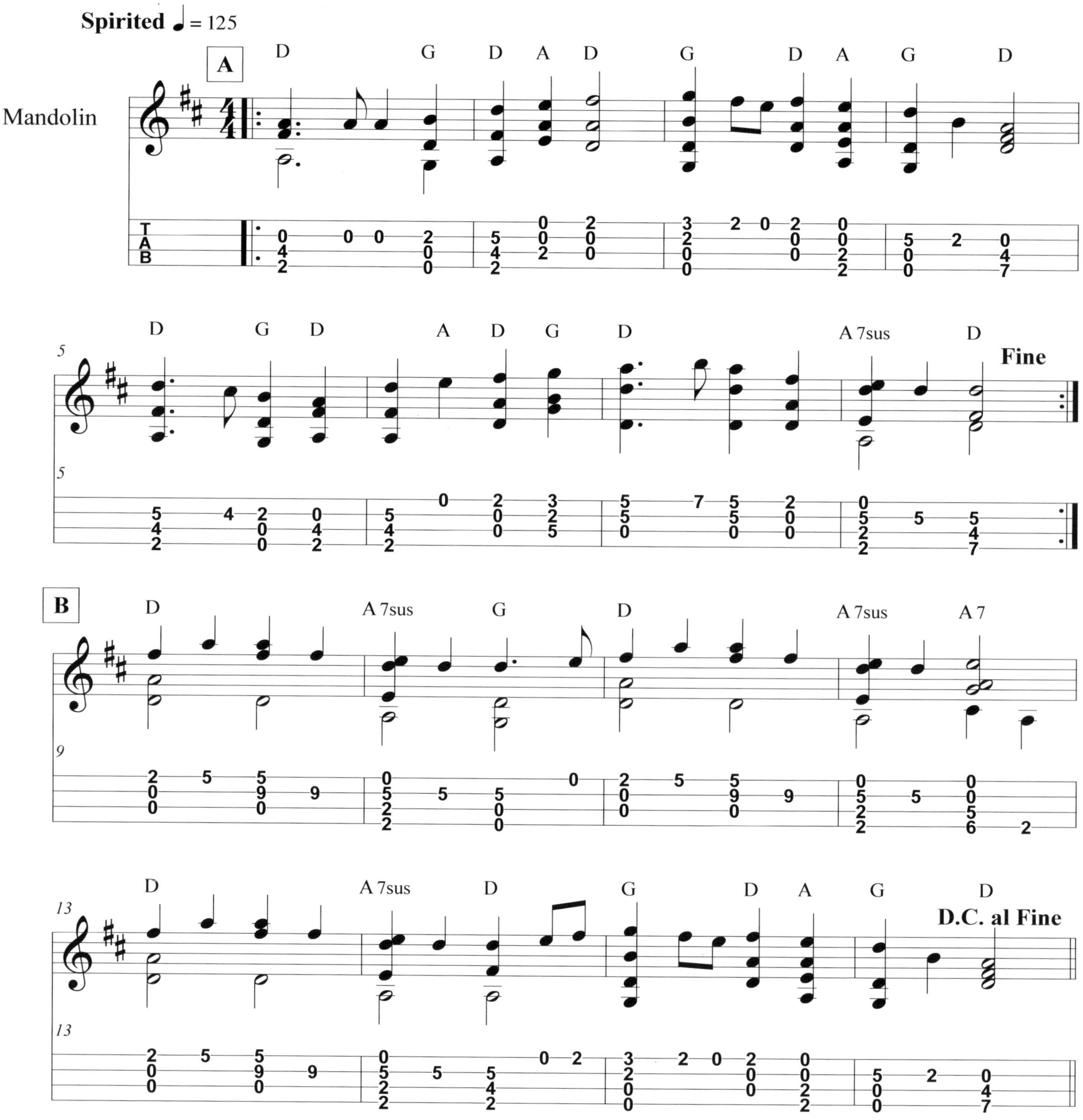

Pigeon on the Fence

Mandolin

Am G

Am G 1. Am

G Am 2. Am G

Am G 1. Am 2. G Am

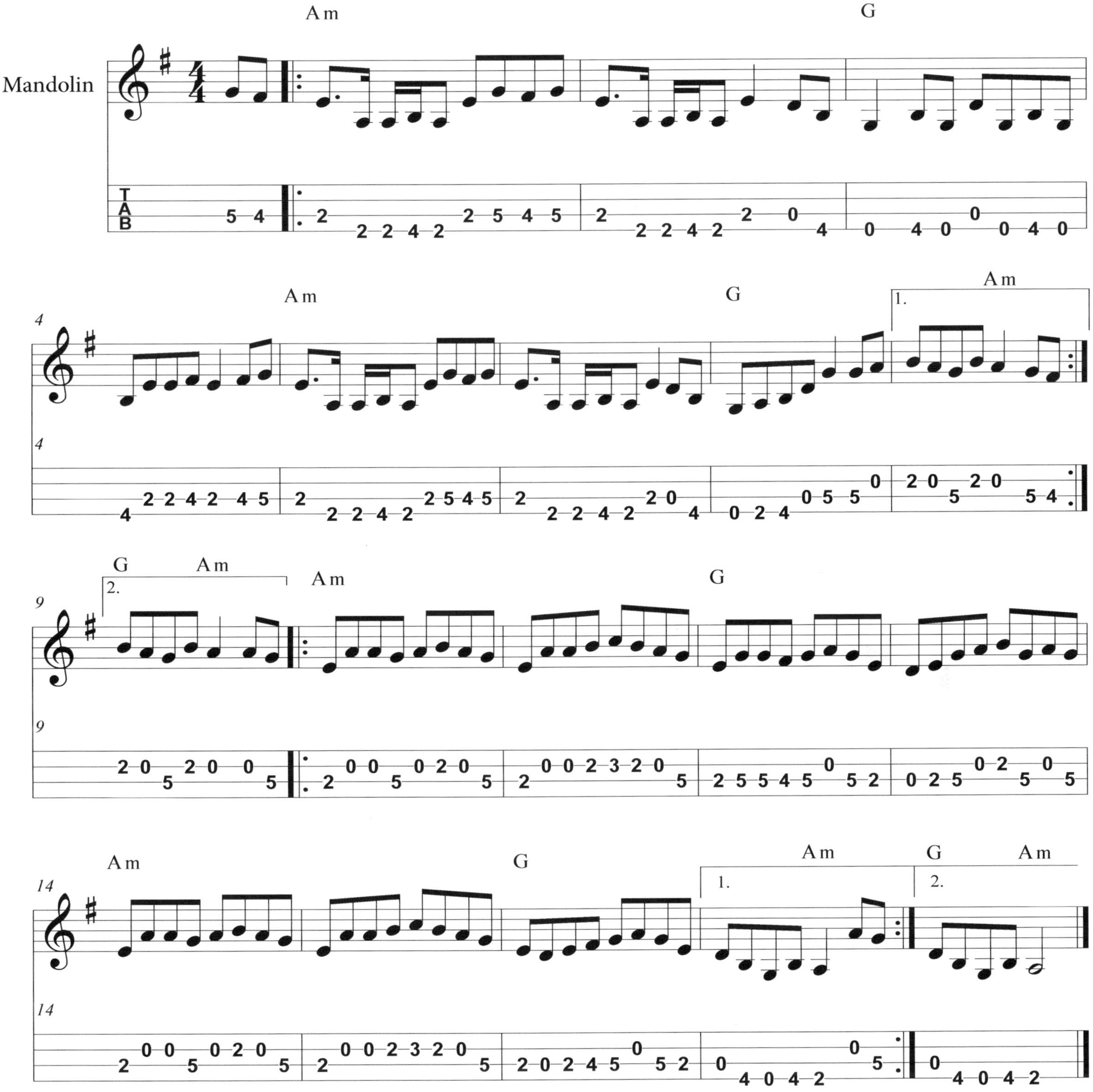

Southwind Waltz

Easy Swing Feeling ♩ = 114

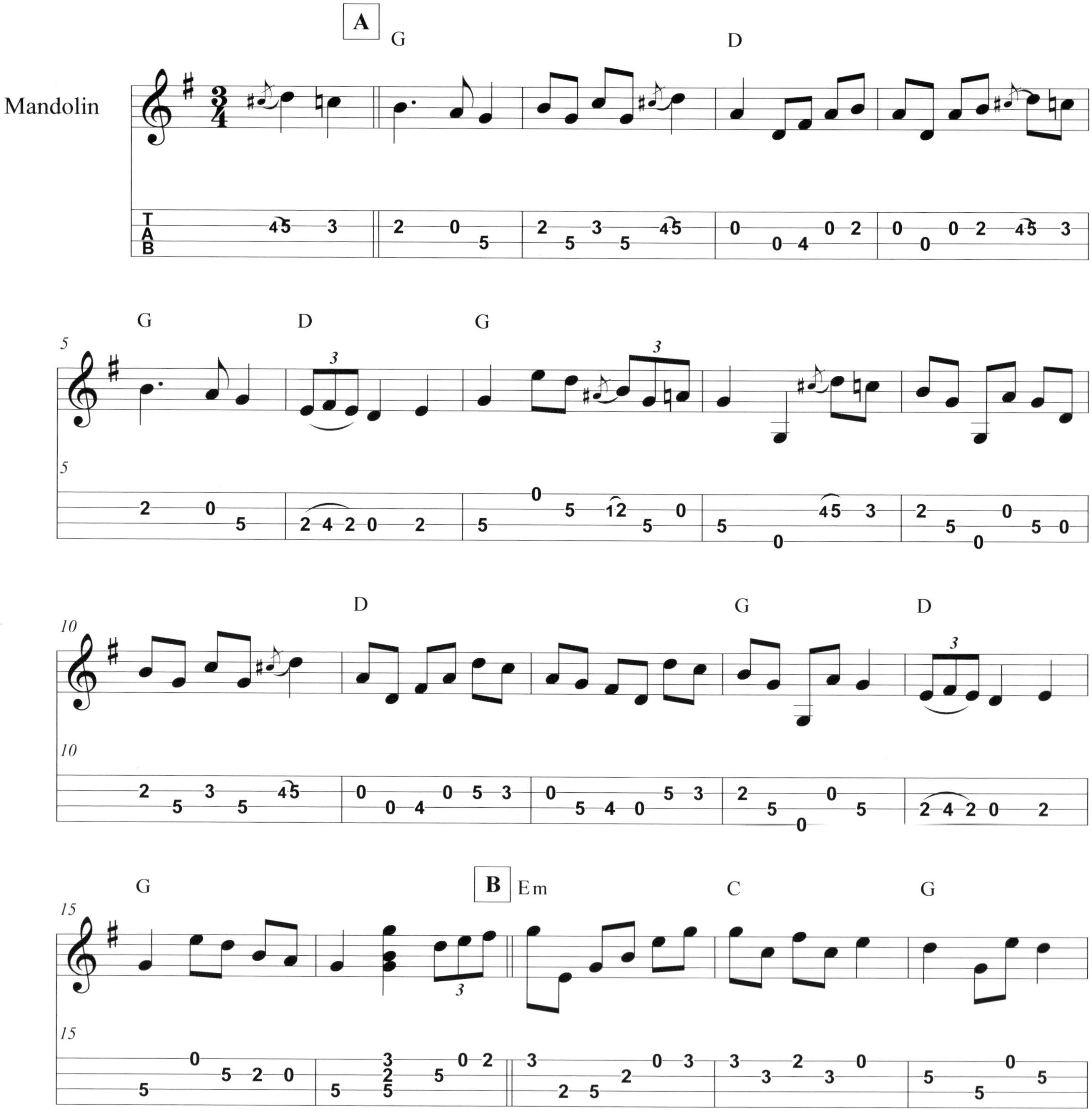

Mandolin

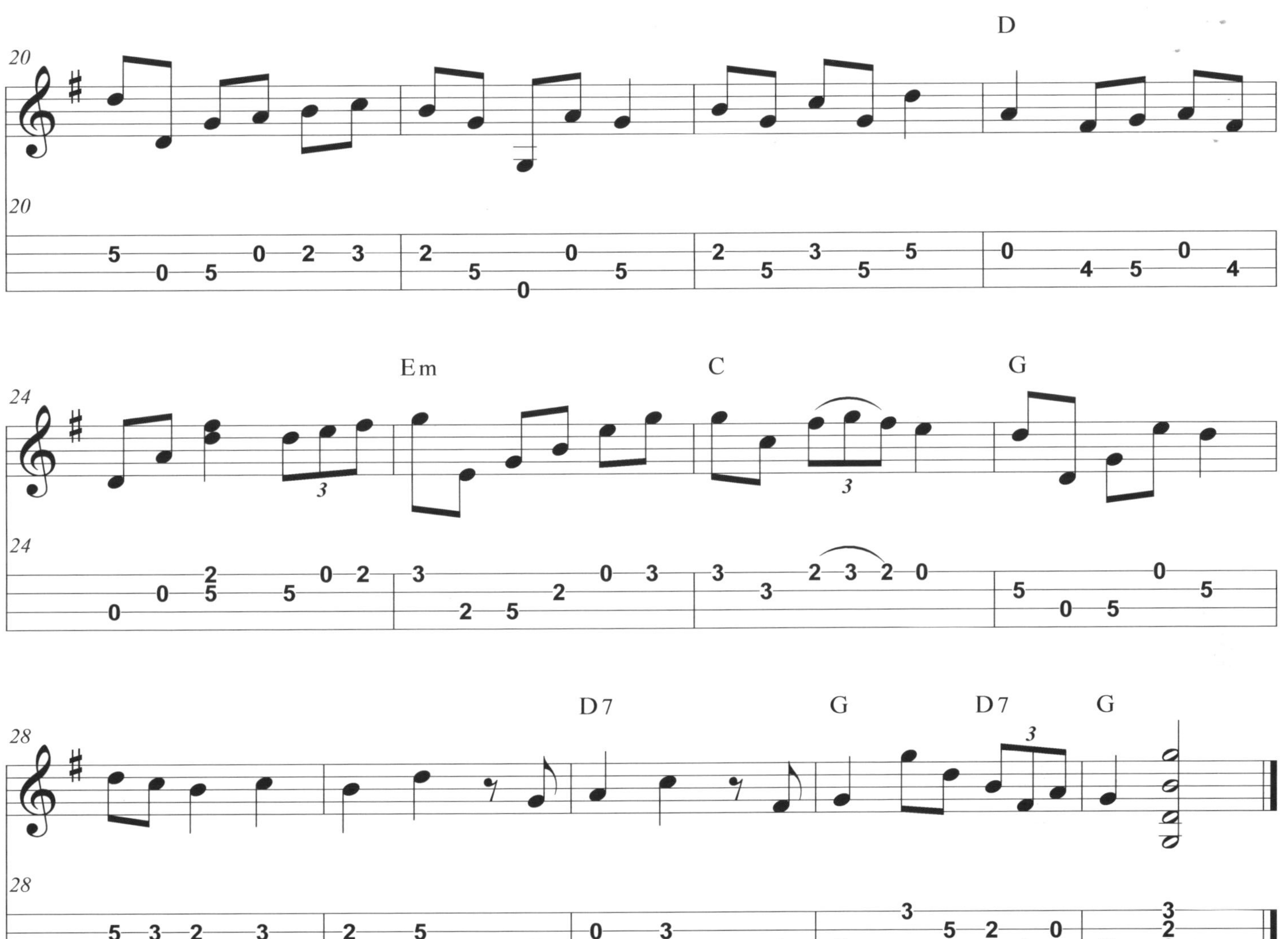
D
Em
C
G
D7
G
D7
G

The Bonny Light Horseman

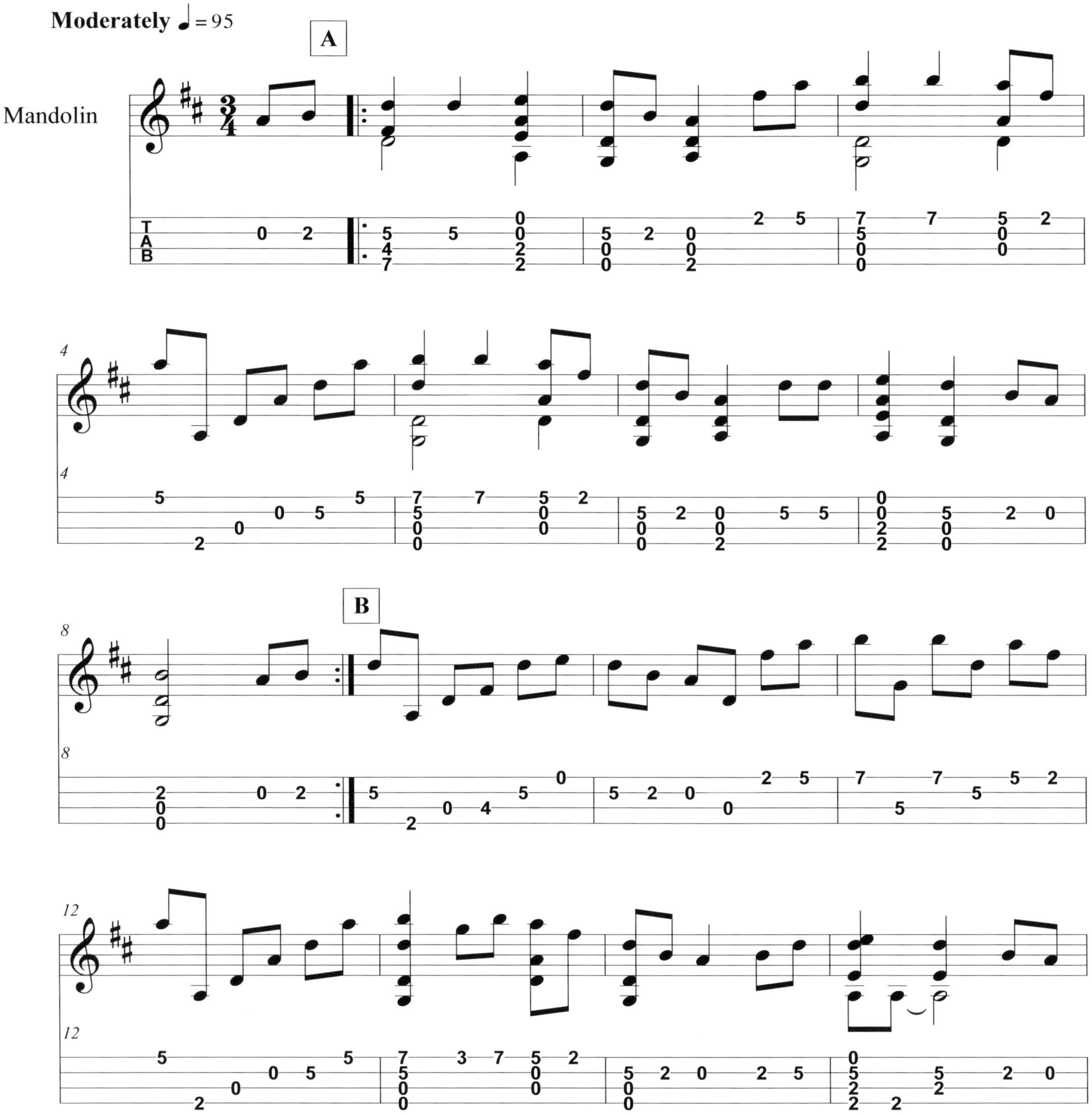

Moderately ♩ = 95

A

Mandolin

T
A
B

B

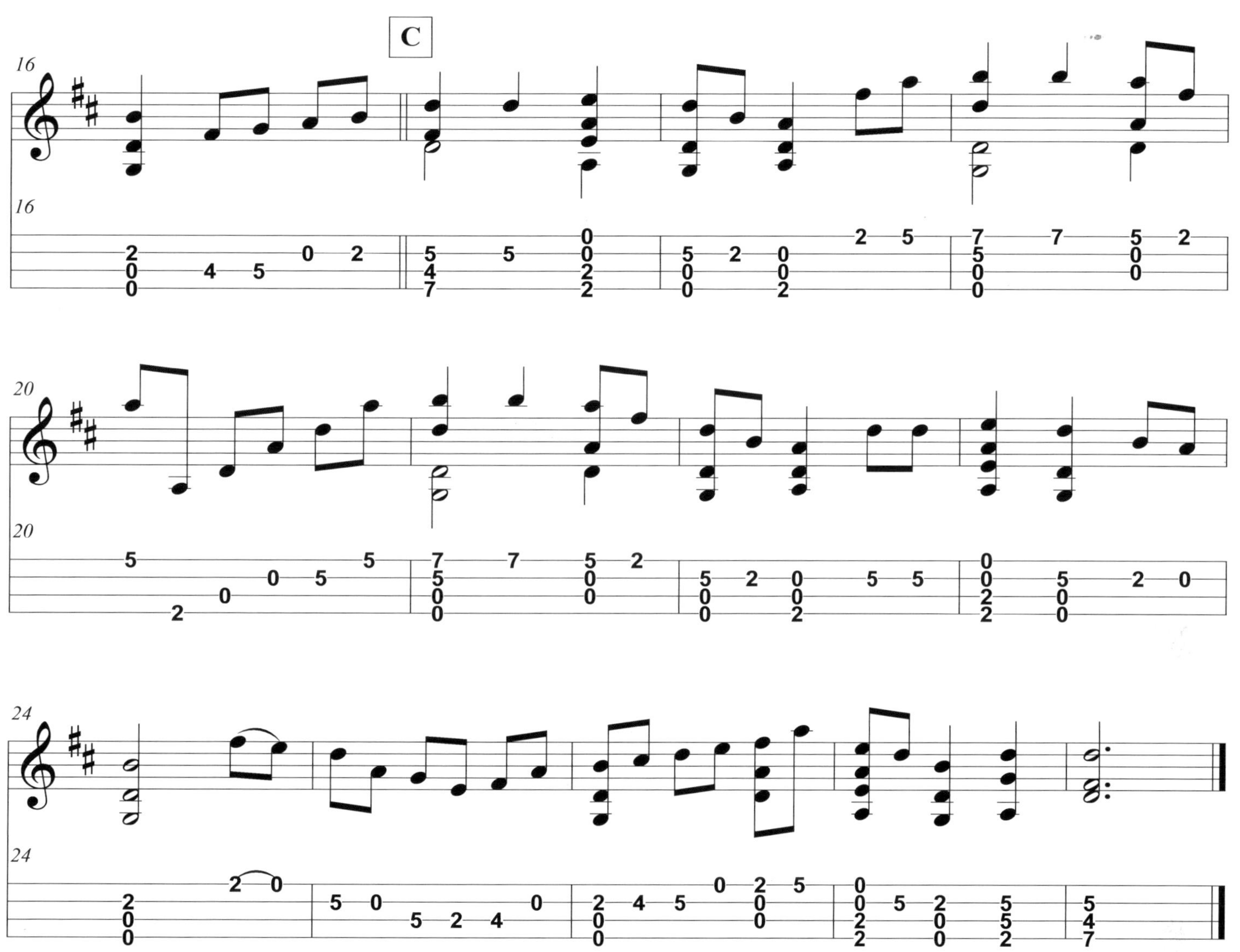
16
C
20
24

The Brave Lad

Rhythmically ♩ = 100

William Bay

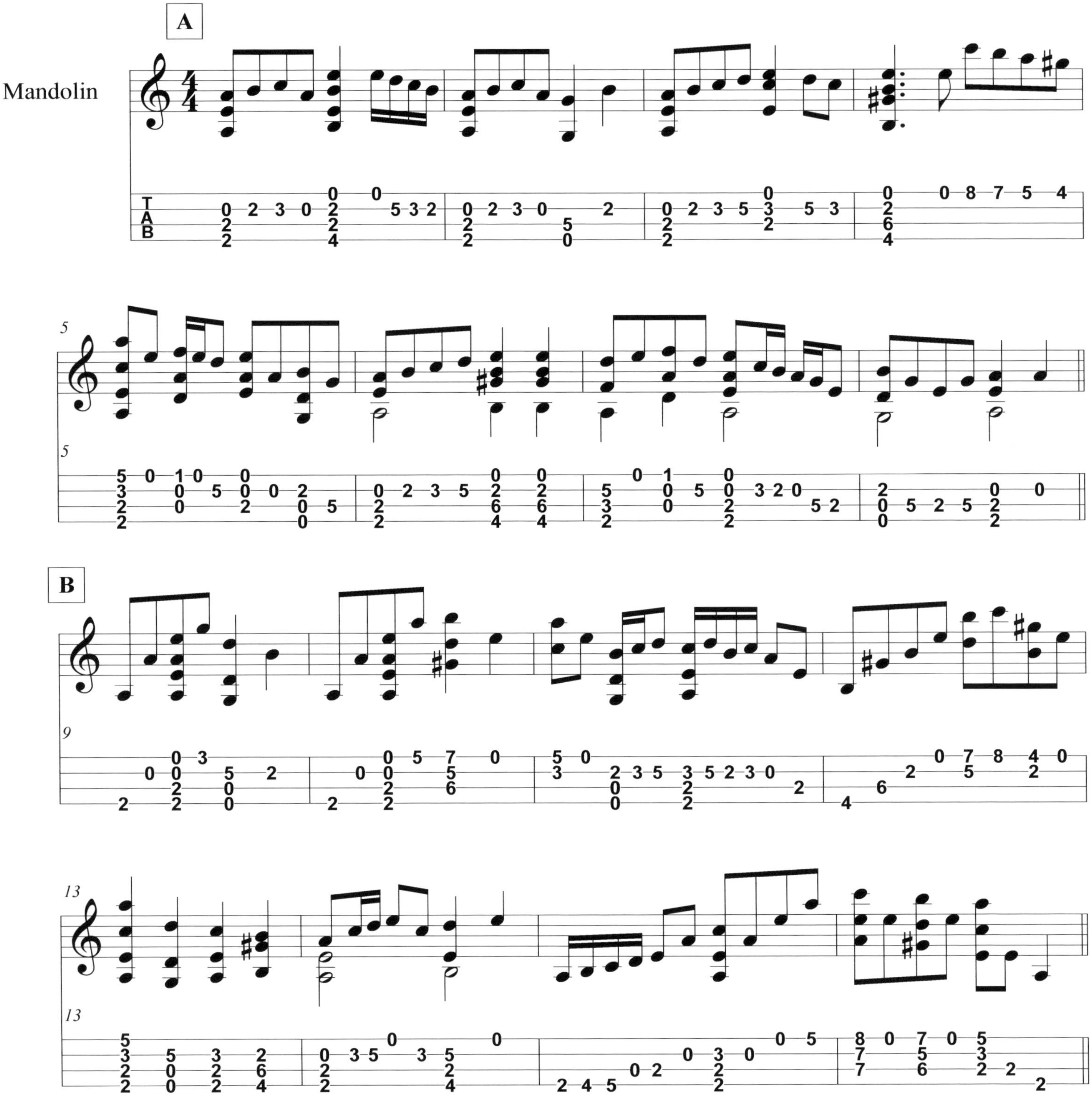

A

Mandolin

B

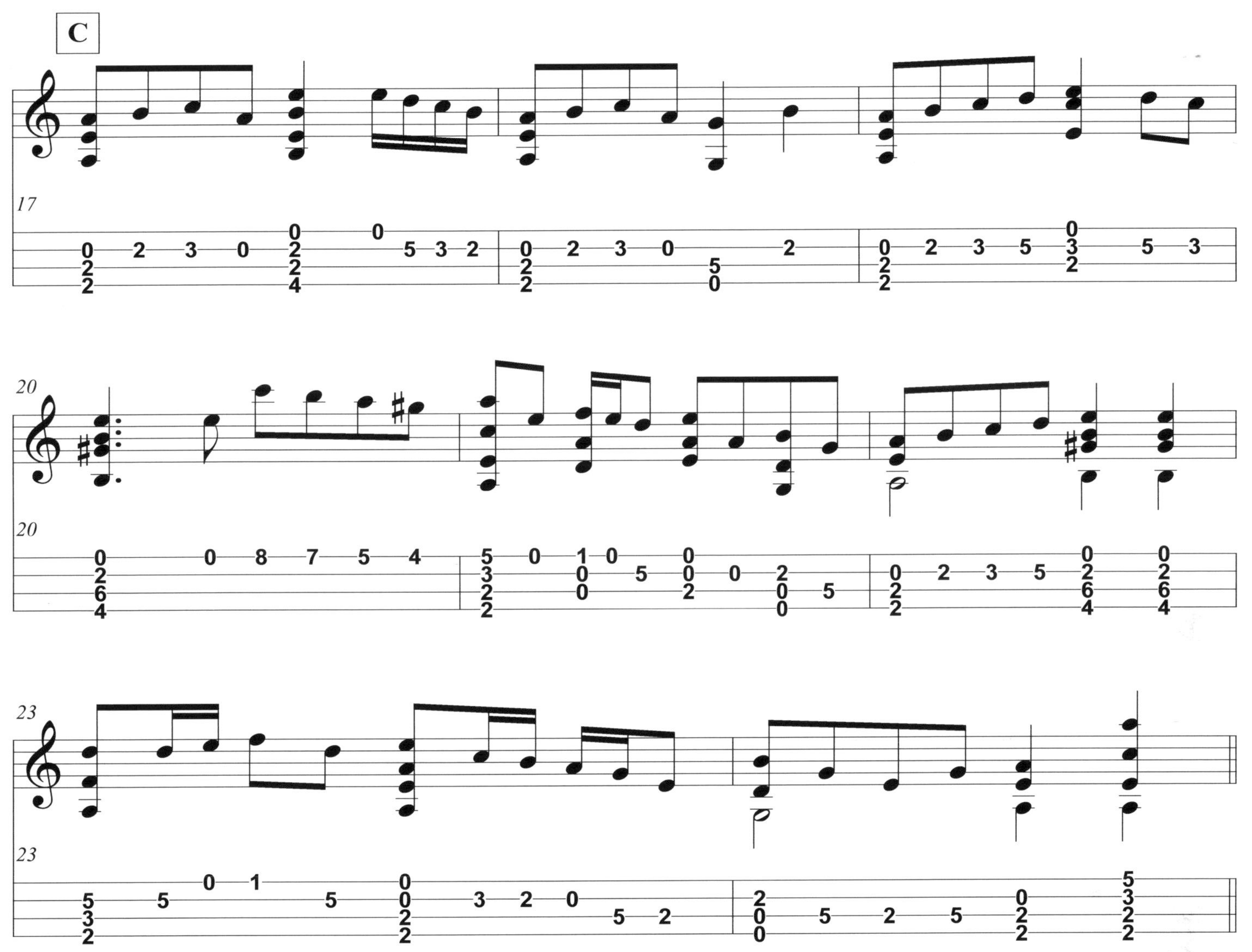
C
17
0 2 3 0 0 0 5 3 2
2 2
2 4
0 2 3 0 2
2 5
2 0
0 2 3 5 0 5 3
2 3
2 2
20
0 0 8 7 5 4
2
6
4
5 0 1 0 0
3 0 5 0 0 2
2 0 2 0 5
2 0
0 2 3 5 0 0
2 2 2
2 6 6
4 4
23
0 1
5 5 5 0
3 0 3 2 0
2 2 5 2
2
2 5
2 5 2 5 0 3
0 2 2
0 2 2

The Boys of Ballisodare

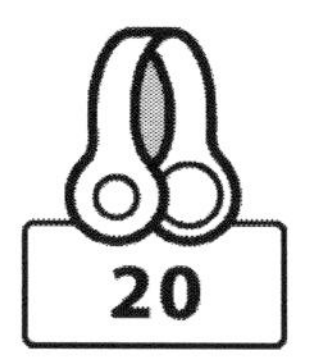

Slip Jig ♩. = 108

A

Mandolin

G Em Bm C G C G Em

G Em Bm C G Em Bm C G Em

B

A5 G C A5 G Am G Em A5 G

G C G Em Bm Am G Em Am G Em

1. 2.

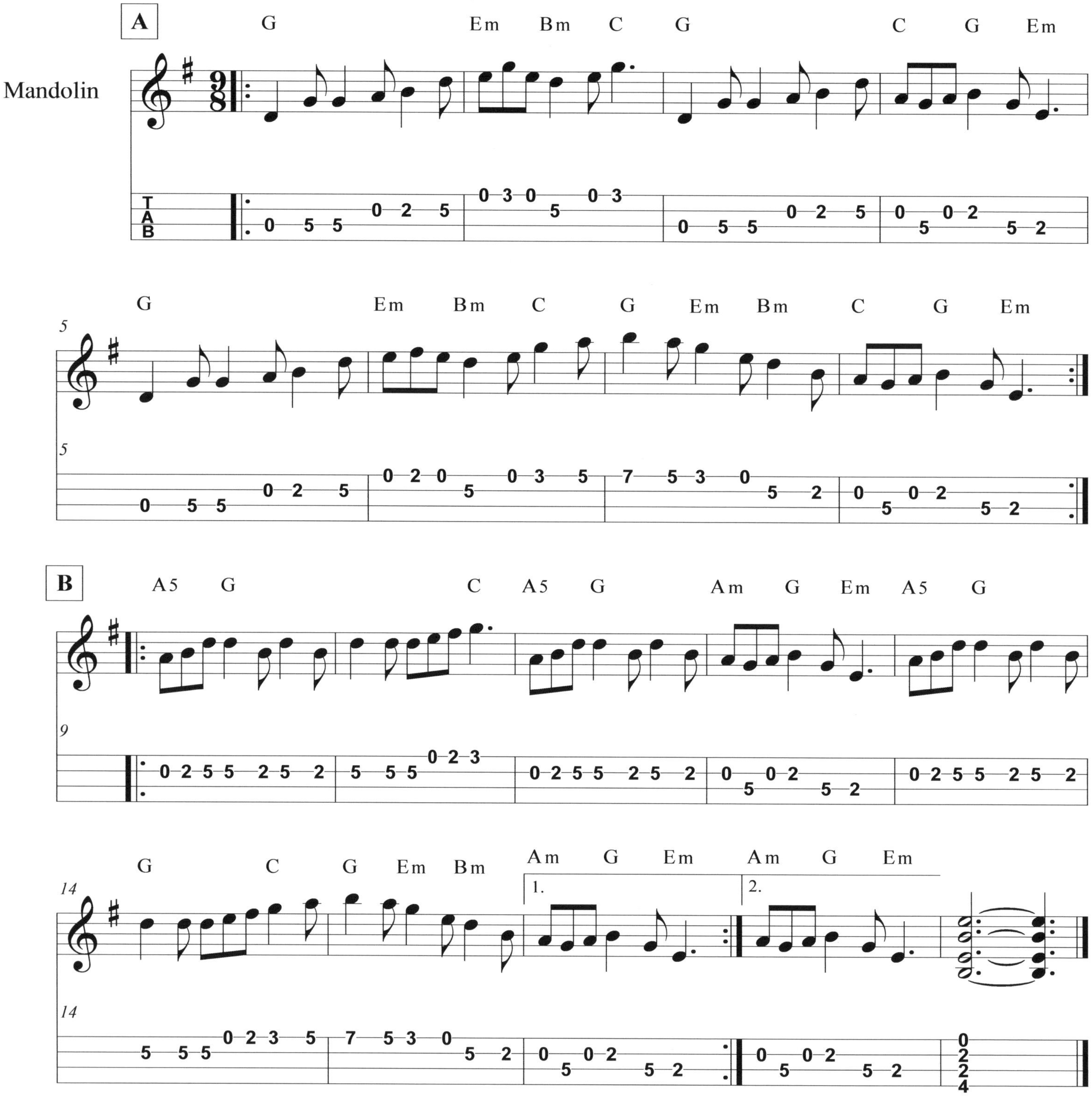

The Connachtman's Rambles

Dance Tempo ♩. = 106

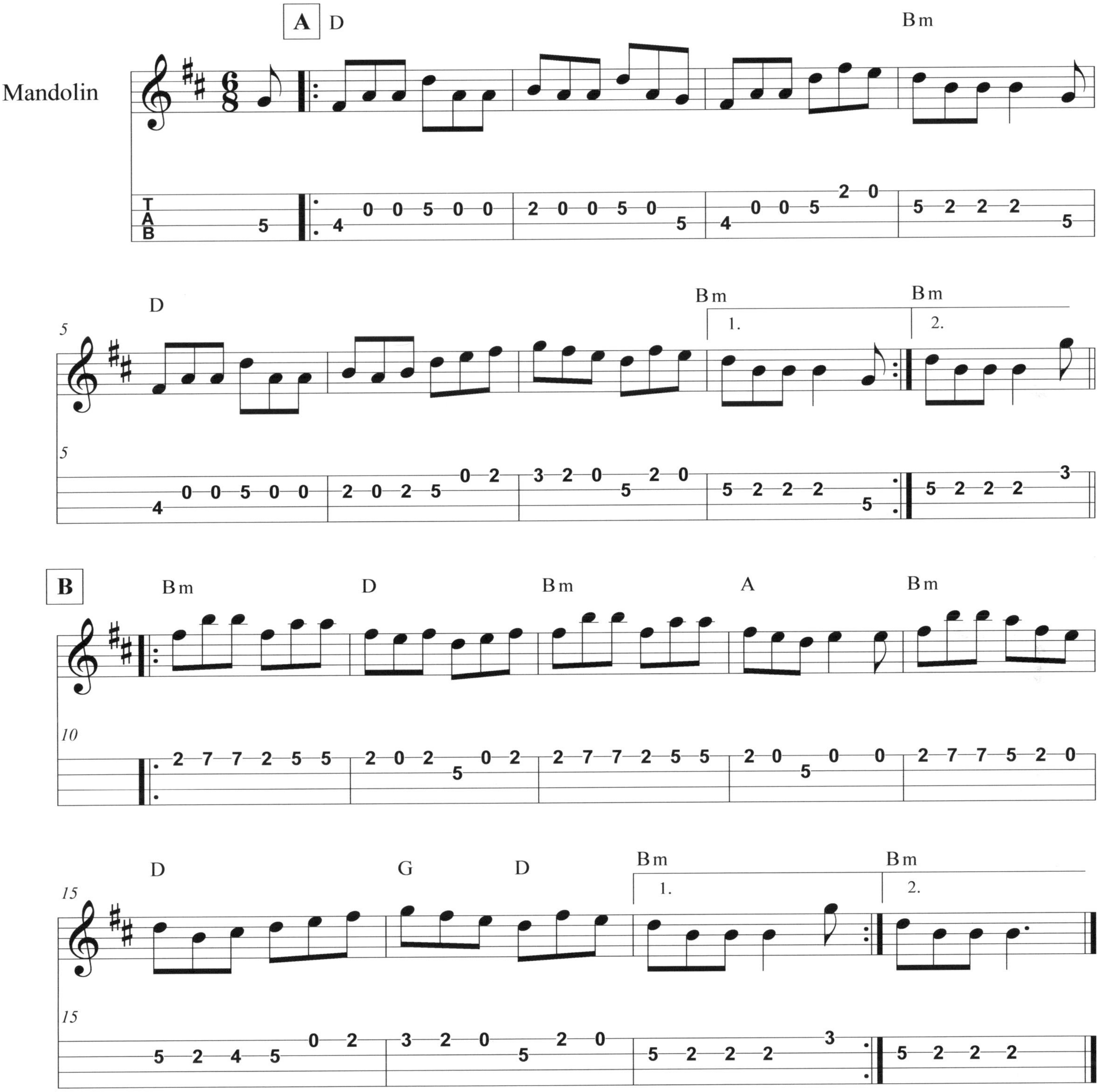

Mandolin

A D Bm

D Bm 1. Bm 2.

B Bm D Bm A Bm

D G D Bm 1. Bm 2.

The Highlander

Rhythmically ♩ = 80

William Bay

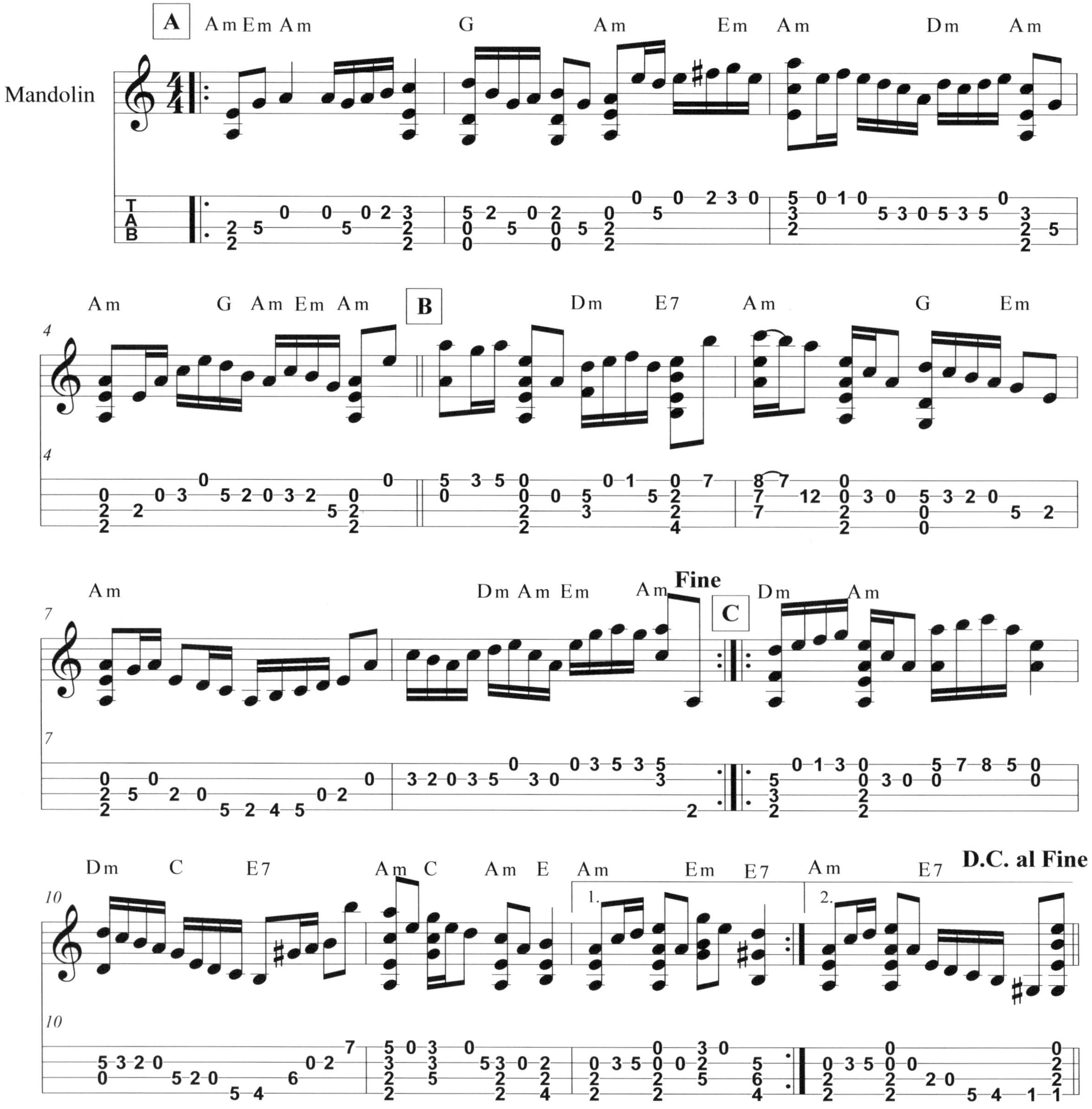

Mandolin

A Am Em Am | G Am Em | Am Dm Am

4 Am G Am Em Am | **B** Dm E7 | Am G Em

7 Am | Dm Am Em Am **Fine** | **C** Dm Am

10 Dm C E7 | Am C Am E | 1. Am Em E7 | 2. Am E7 **D.C. al Fine**

The Lilting Banshee

Dance Tempo ♩. = 102

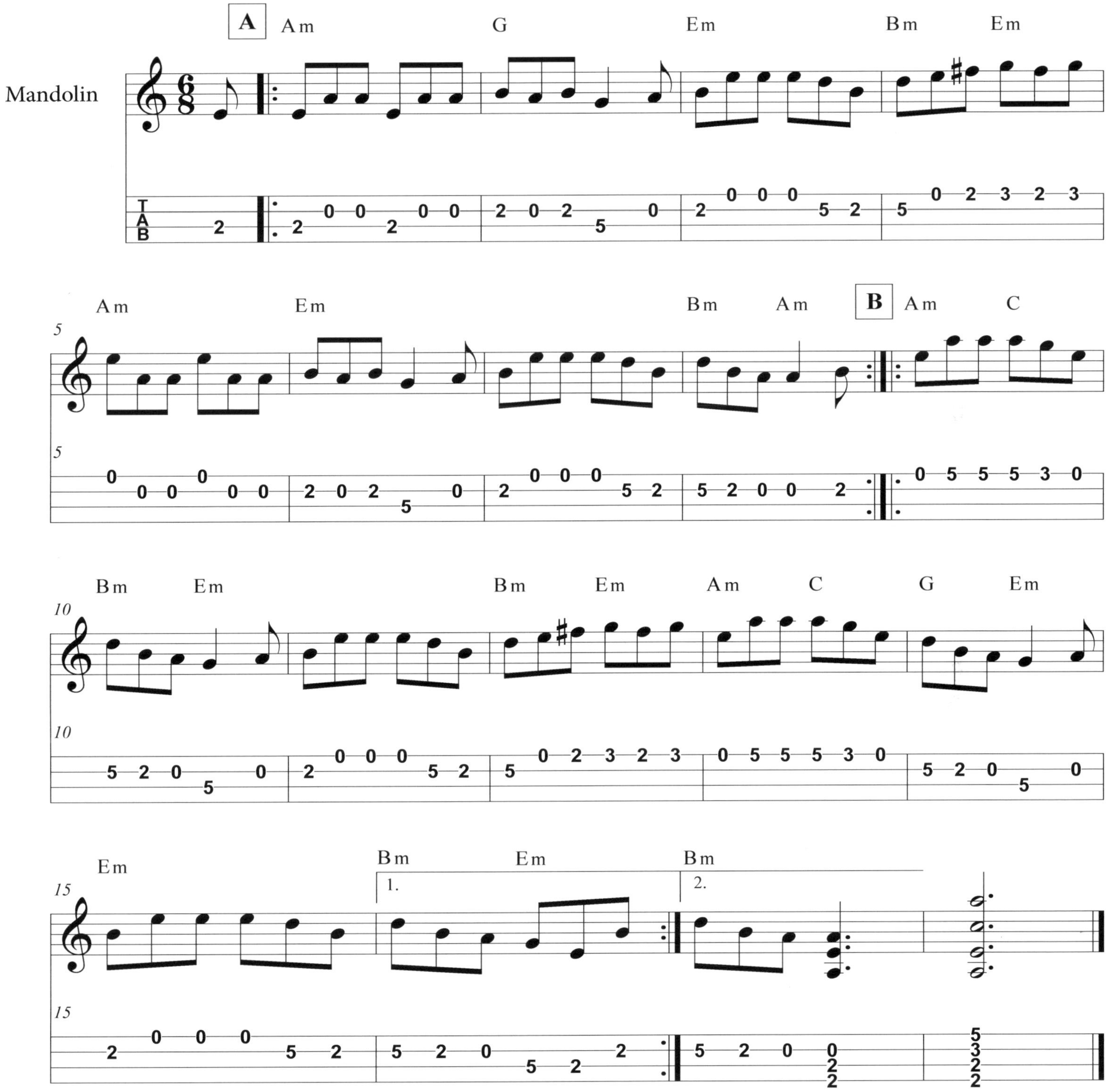

Mandolin

A — Am, G, Em, Bm, Em

Am, Em, Bm, Am

B — Am, C

Bm, Em, Bm, Em, Am, C, G, Em

Em, Bm, Em (1.), Bm (2.)

The Highwayman's Reel

Lively Tempo ♩ = 112

William Bay

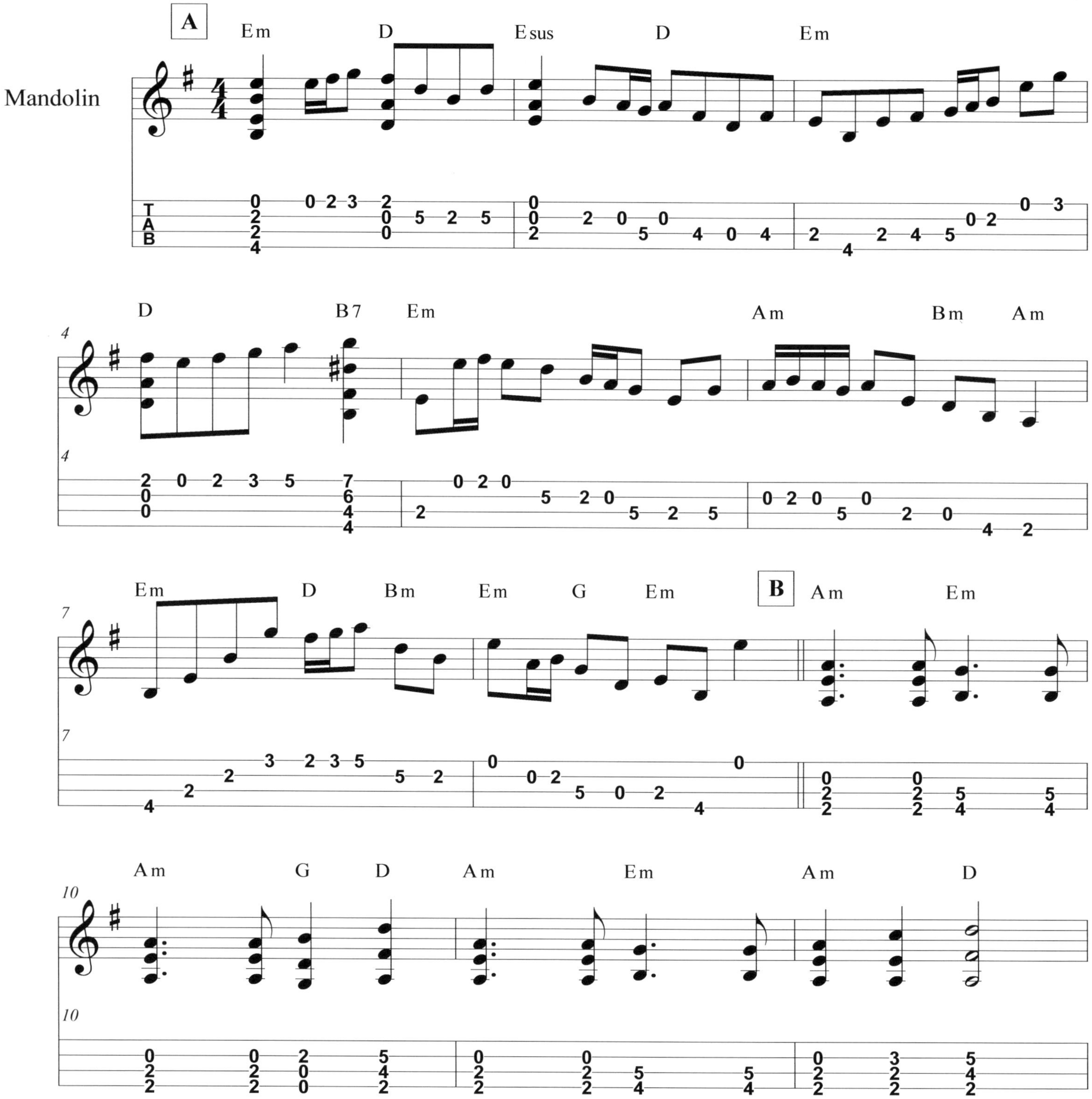

Mandolin

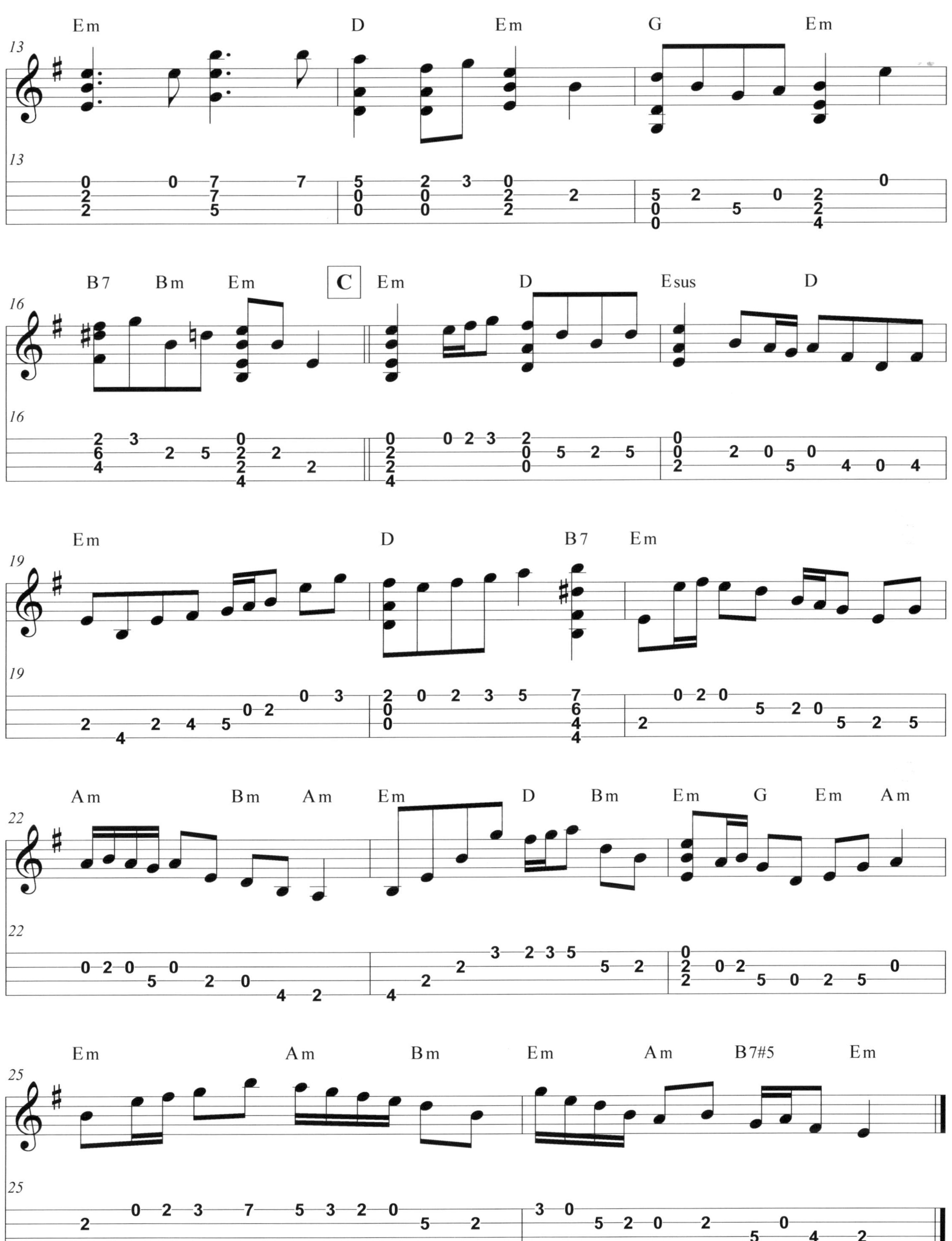
Em D Em G Em
B7 Bm Em C Em D Esus D
Em D B7 Em
Am Bm Am Em D Bm Em G Em Am
Em Am Bm Em Am B7#5 Em

The Lost Child

William Bay

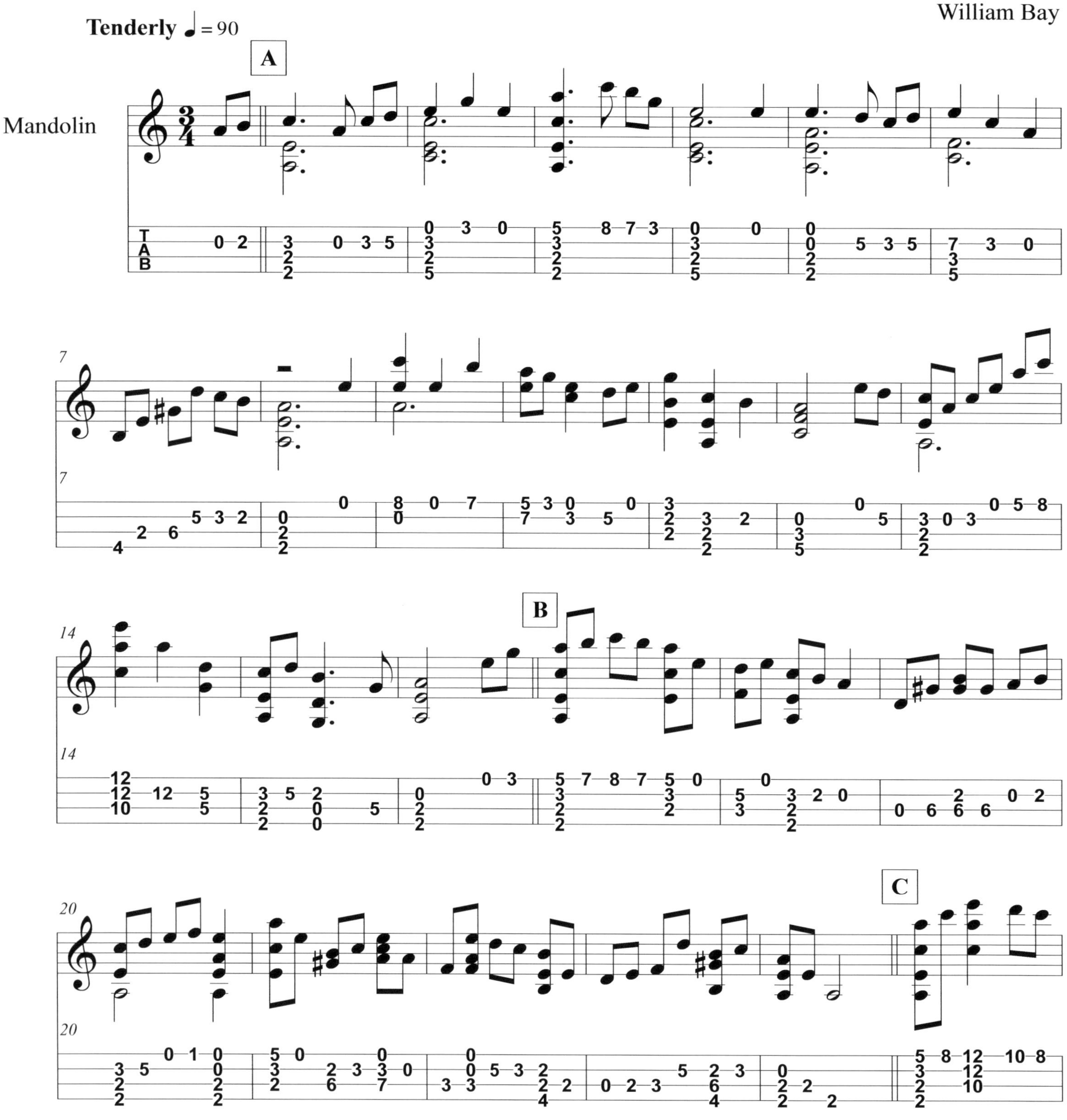

Tenderly ♩ = 90

A

Mandolin

B

C

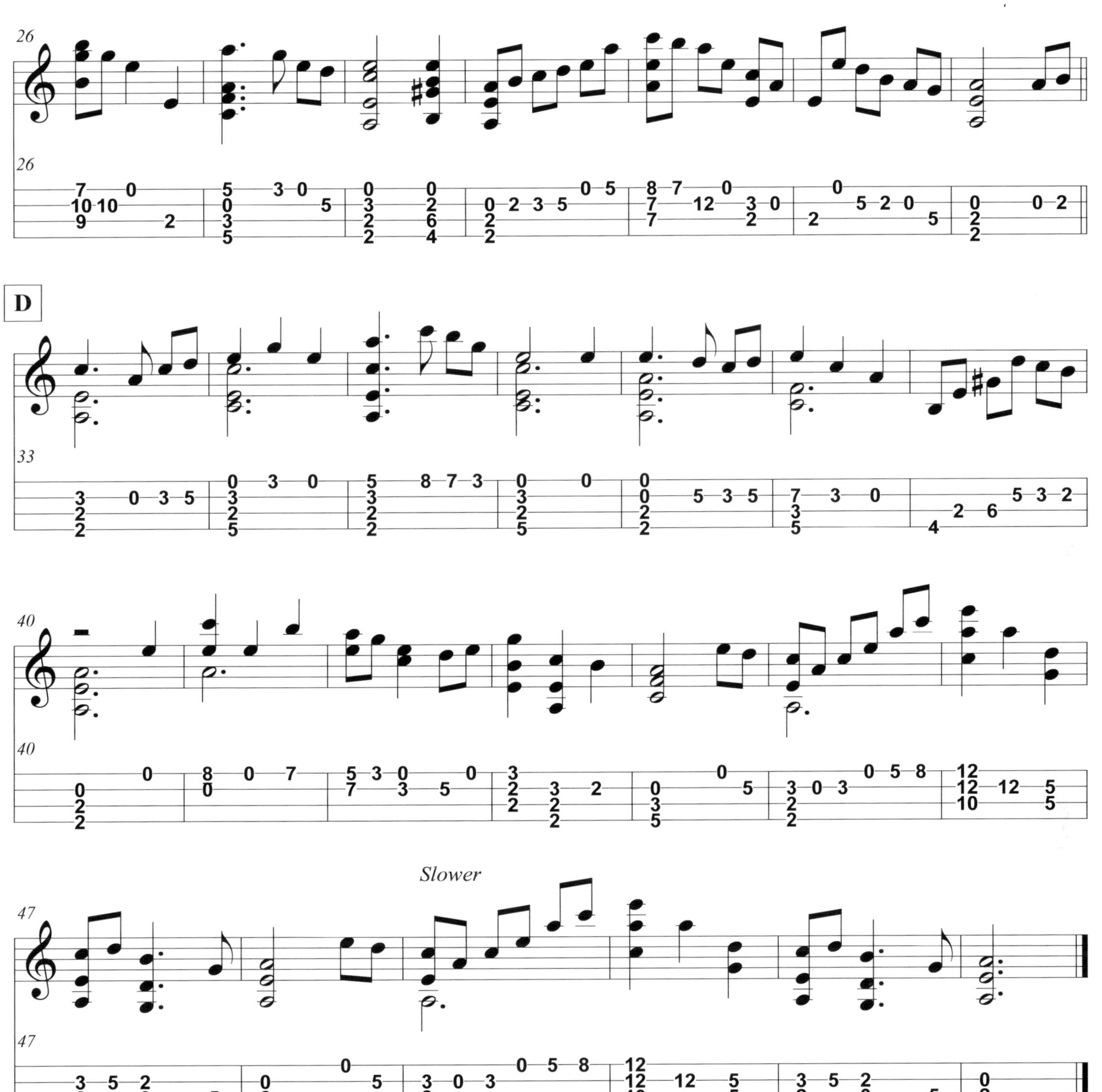
D
Slower

The Mist-Covered Mountains of Home

Ballad

Moderato ♩ = 105

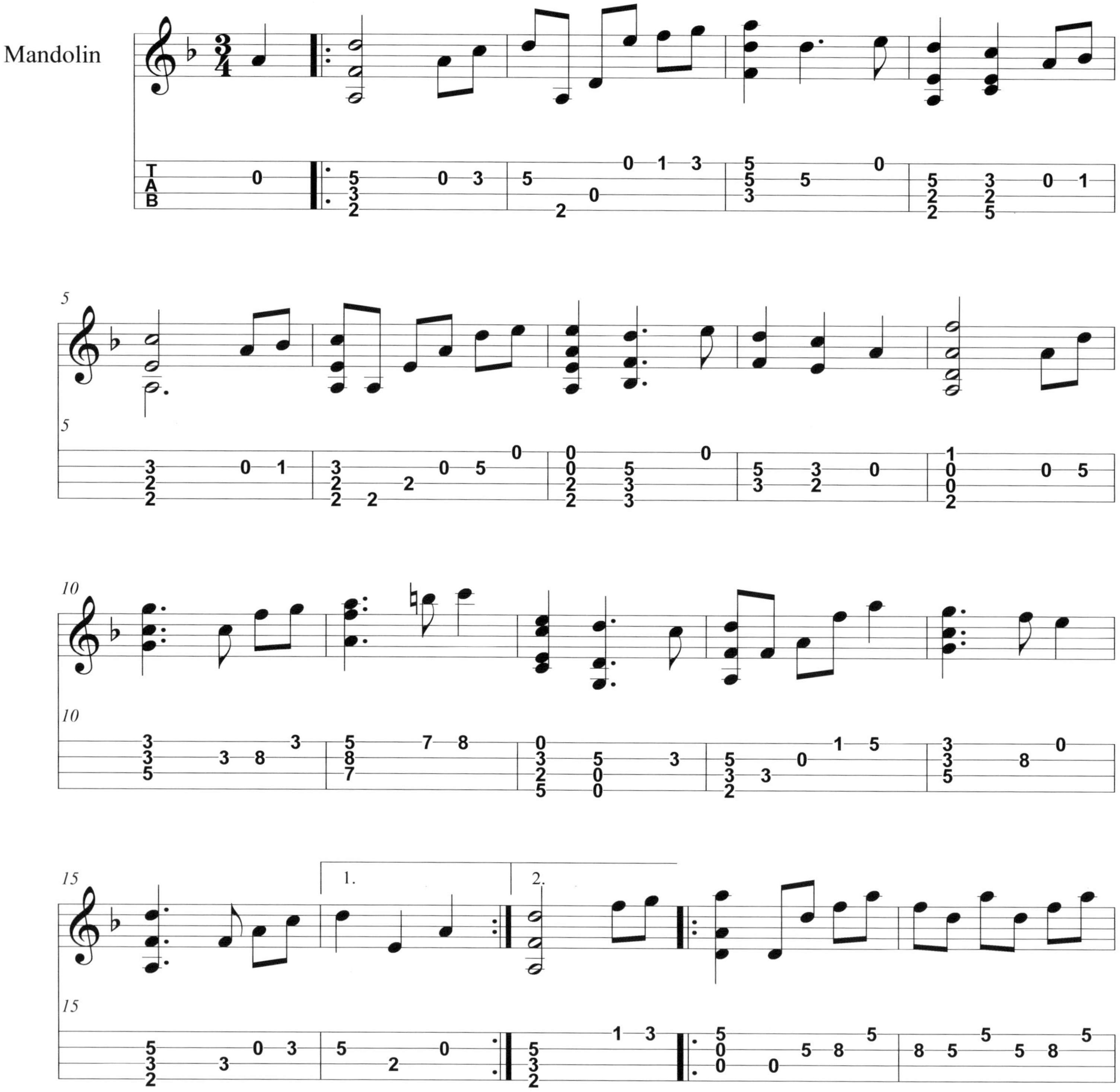

Mandolin

1.

2.

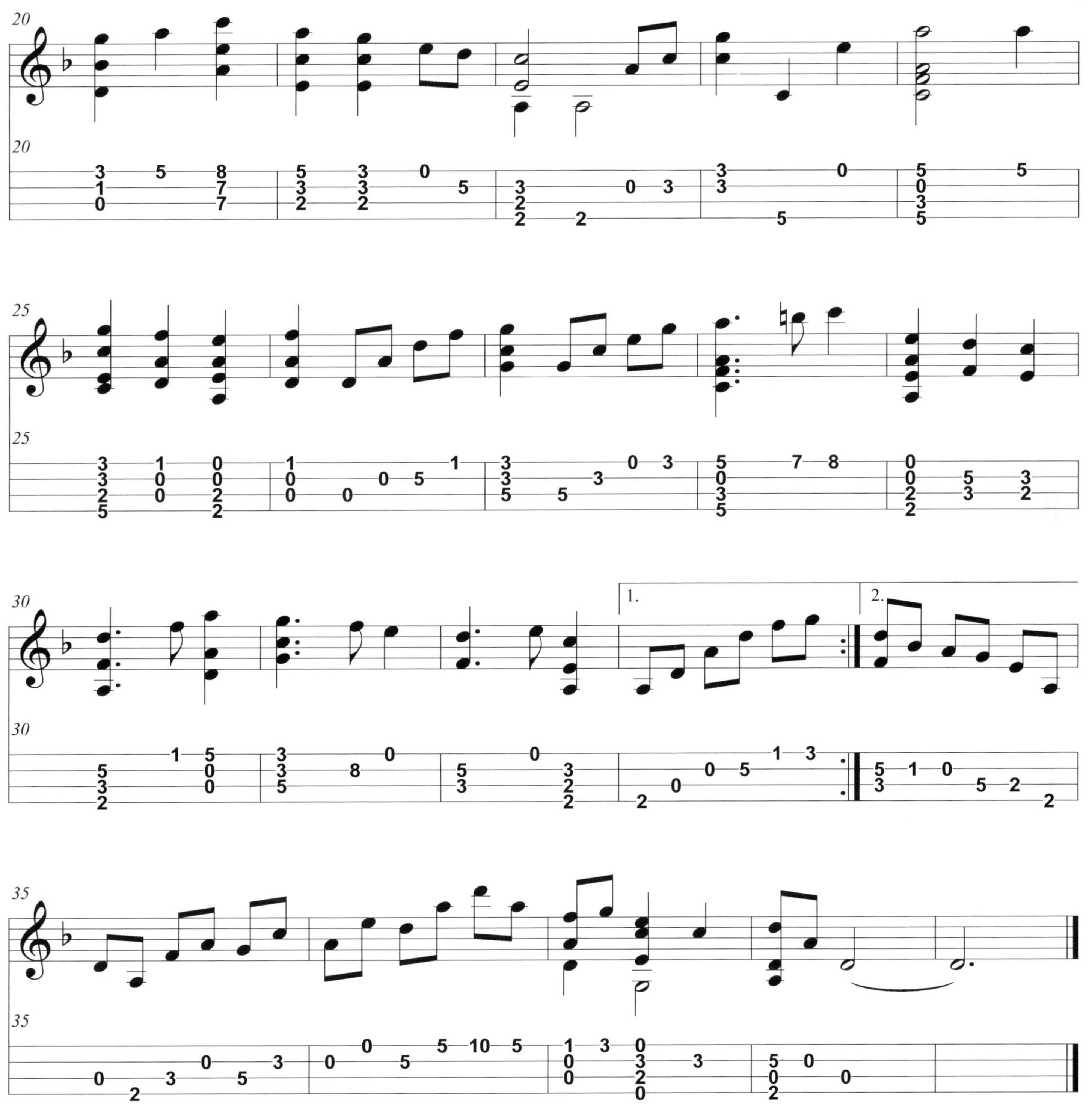

The Rambling Pitchfork

Lively ♩. = 108

Mandolin

A

D G

A7 D G

A7 D B D G

F D G

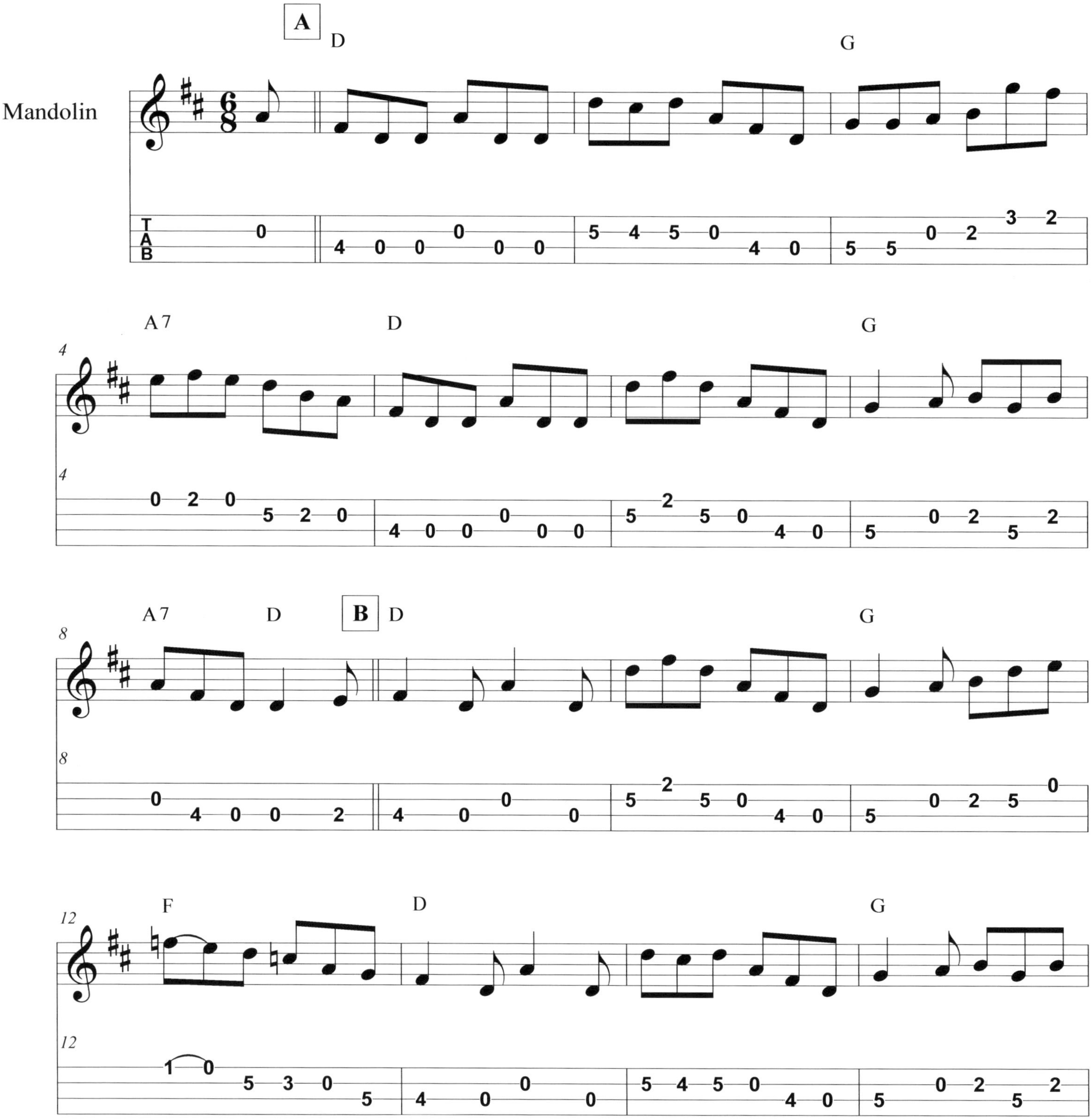

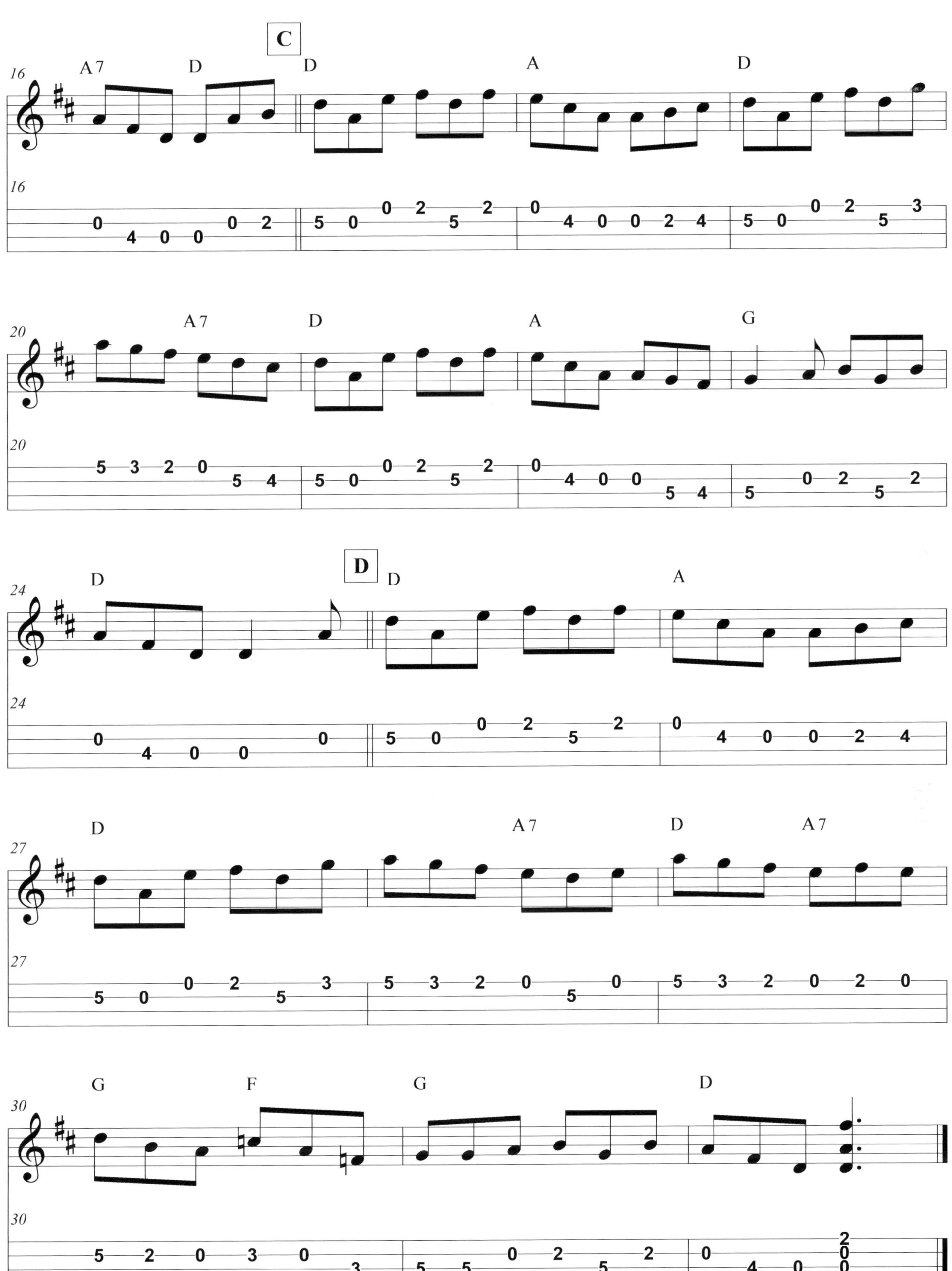
A7
D
C
D
A
D
A7
D
A
G
D
D
D
A
D
A7
D
A7
G
F
G
D

Treasure of My Heart

Moderately ♩ = 100

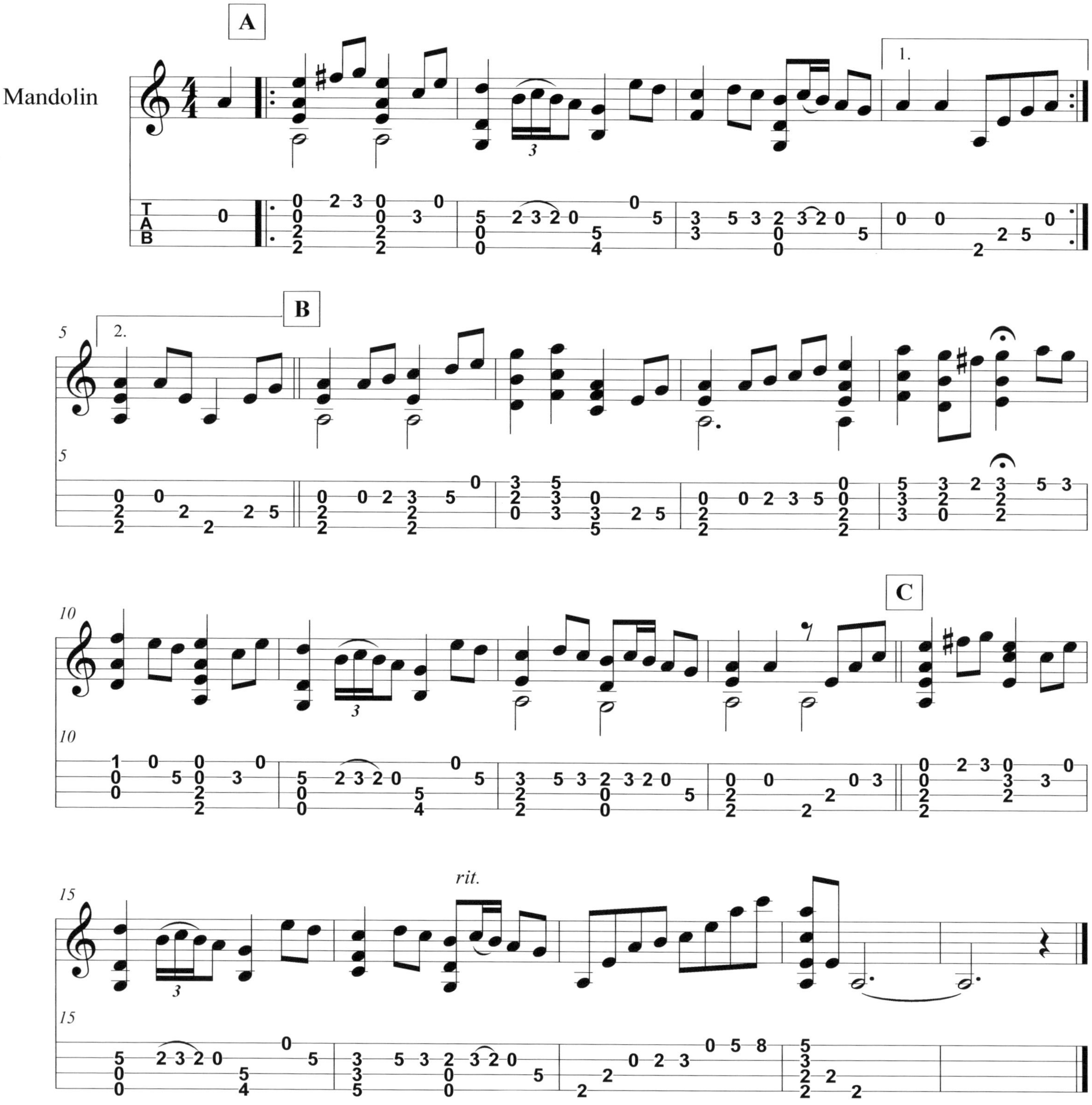

A

Mandolin

TAB

1.

2.

B

C

rit.

Drowsie Maggie

Allegro ♩ = 134

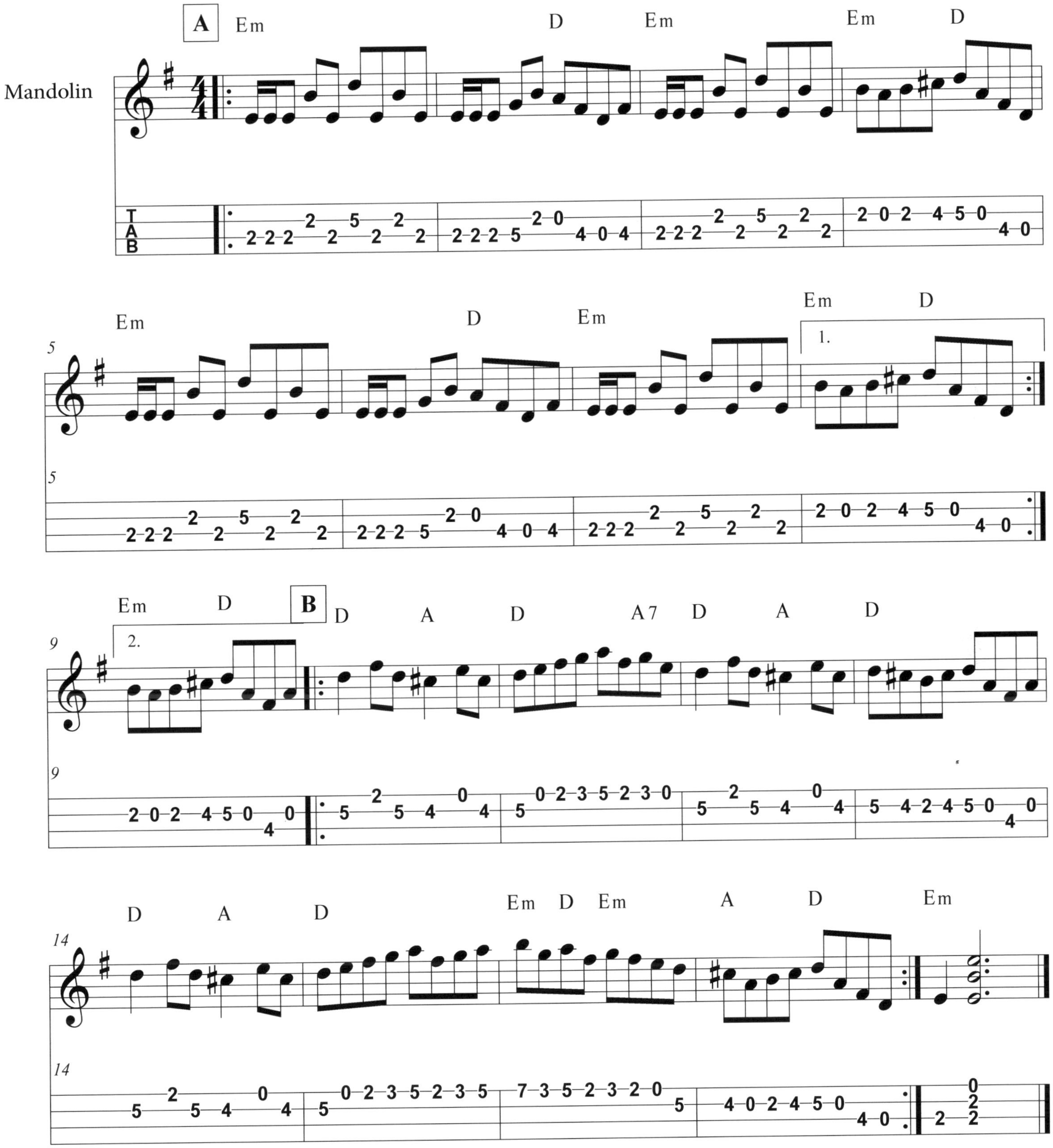

Carolan's Fancy

30

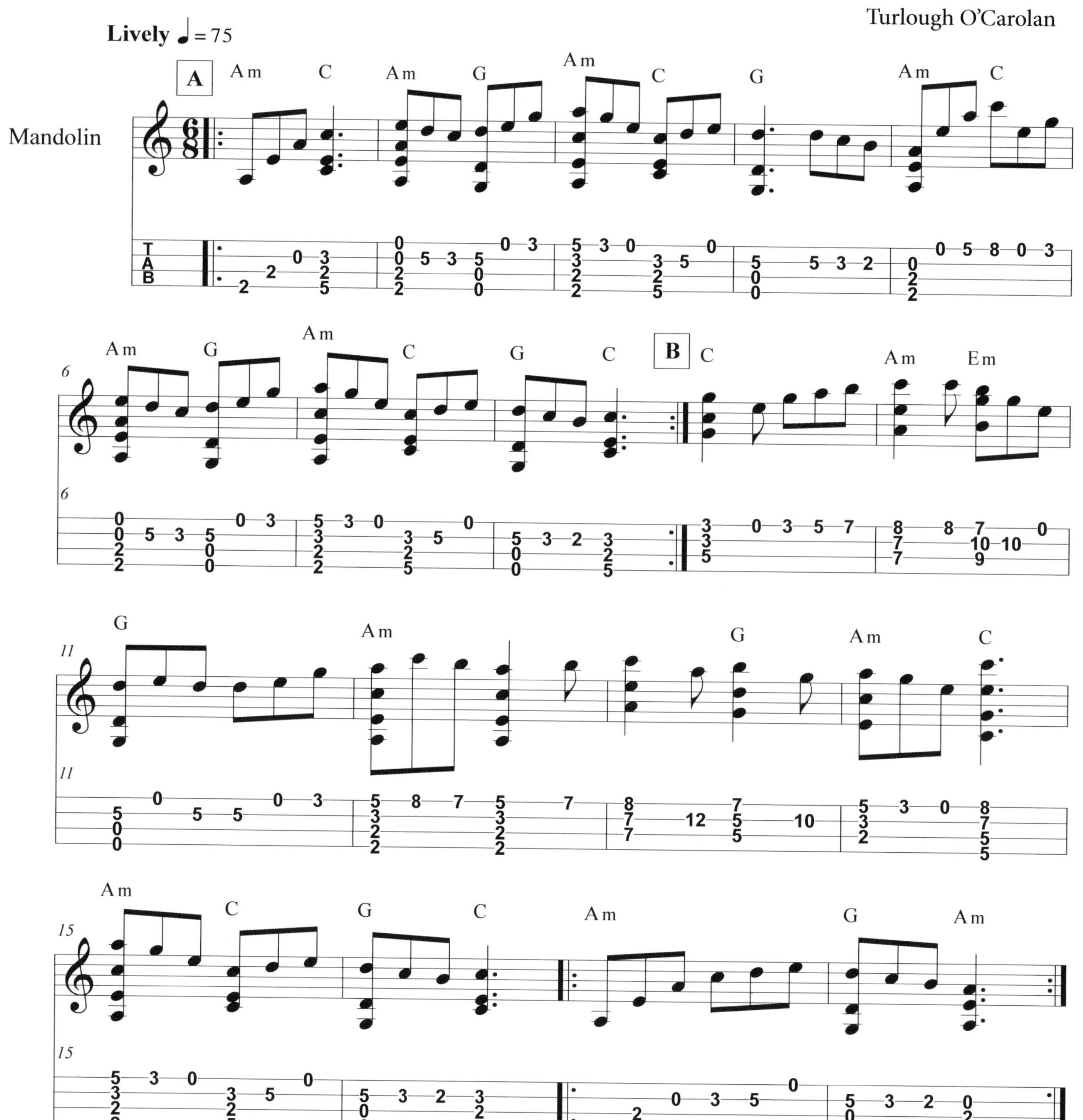

Dundee Hornpipe

31

Moderately 𝅗𝅥 = 80

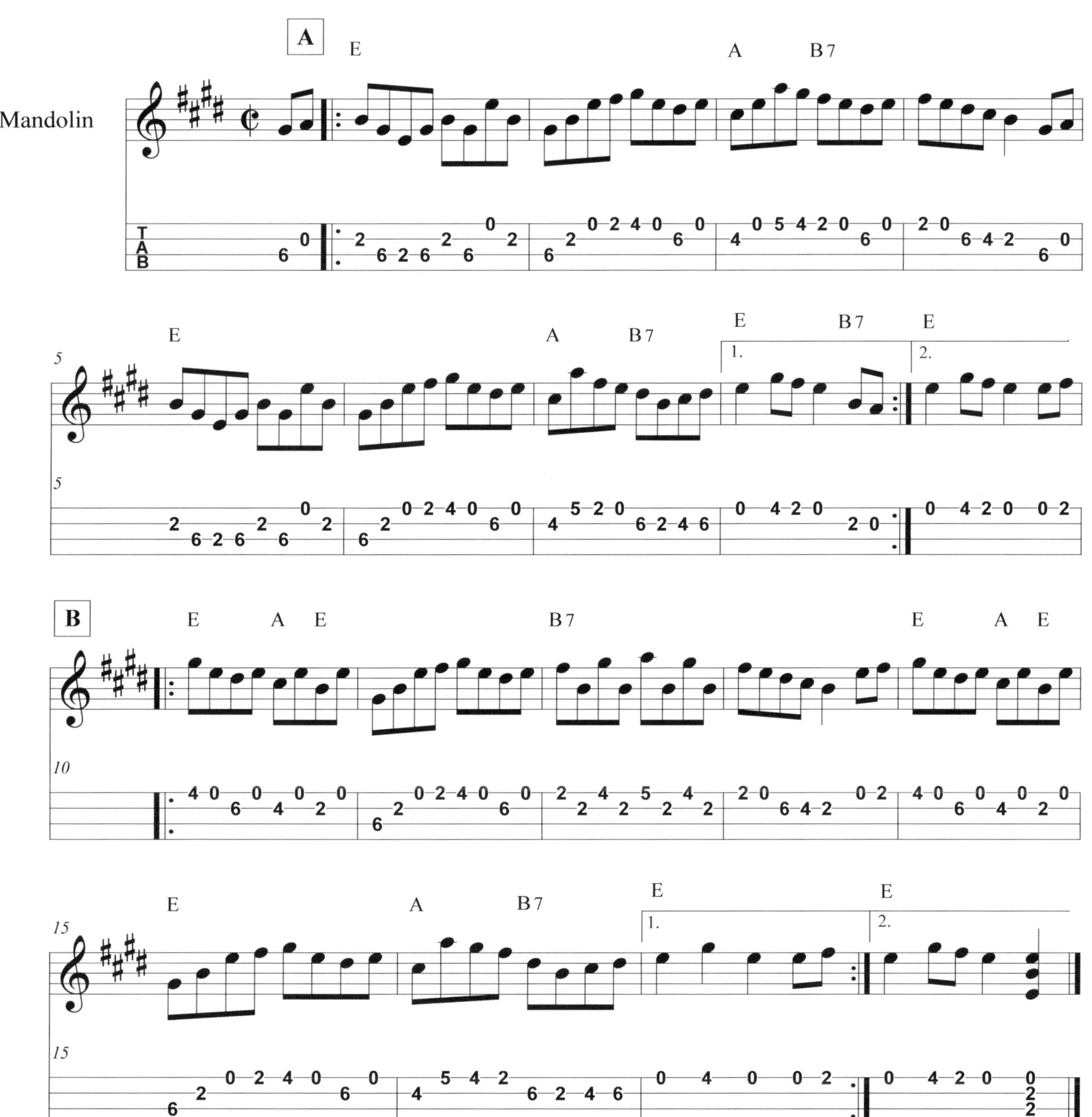

Kiss the Bride Reel

Moderate Swing 𝅗𝅥 = 80

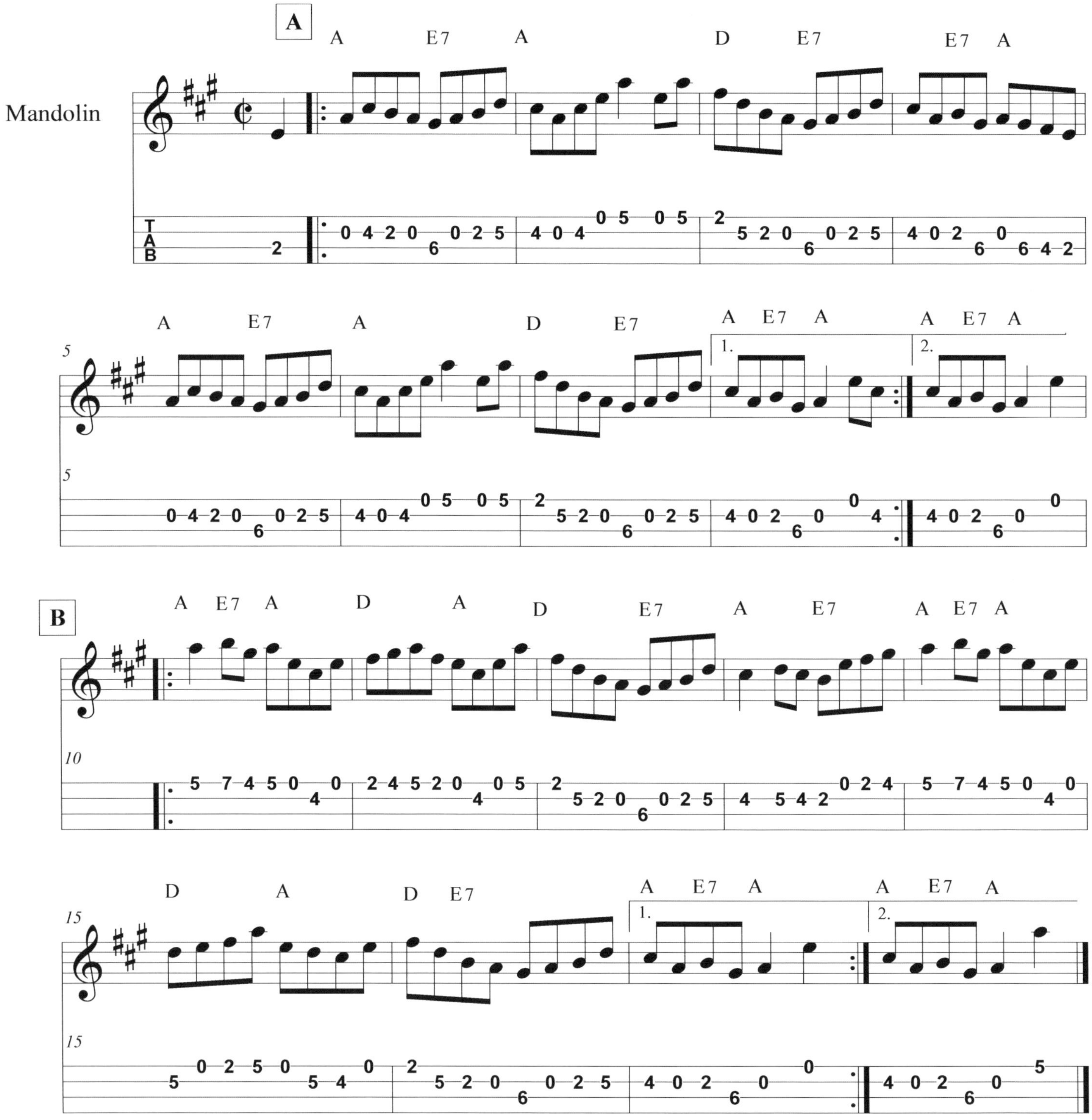

A

Mandolin

A E7 A D E7 E7 A

A E7 A D E7 A E7 A 1. A E7 A 2.

B

A E7 A D A D E7 A E7 A E7 A

D A D E7 A E7 A 1. A E7 A 2.

Maggie Picking Cockels Reel

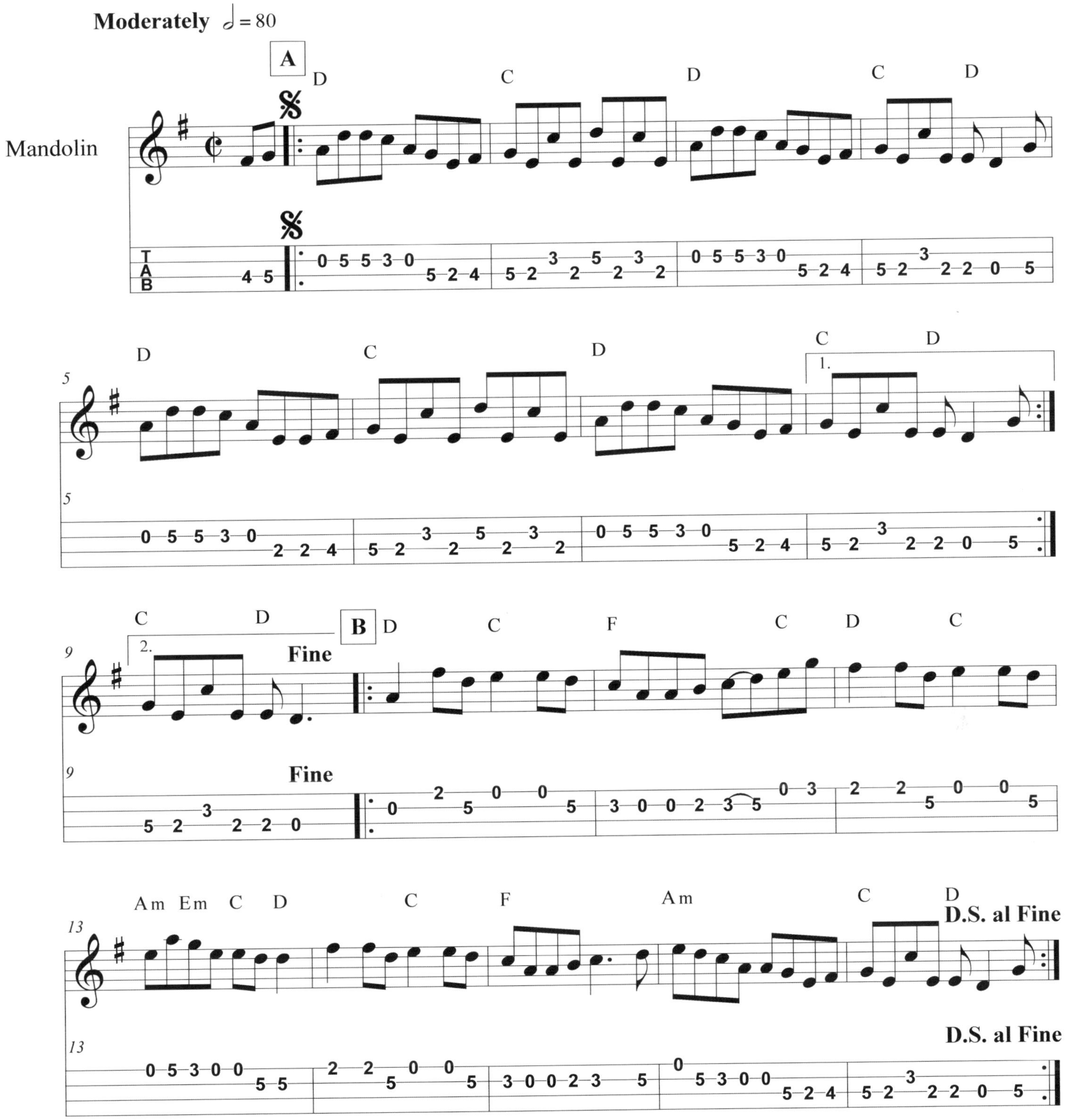

Moderately 𝅗𝅥 = 80

A

Mandolin

D C D C D

D C D C D

1.

C D

2.

Fine

B

D C F C D C

Am Em C D C F Am C D

D.S. al Fine

About the Author

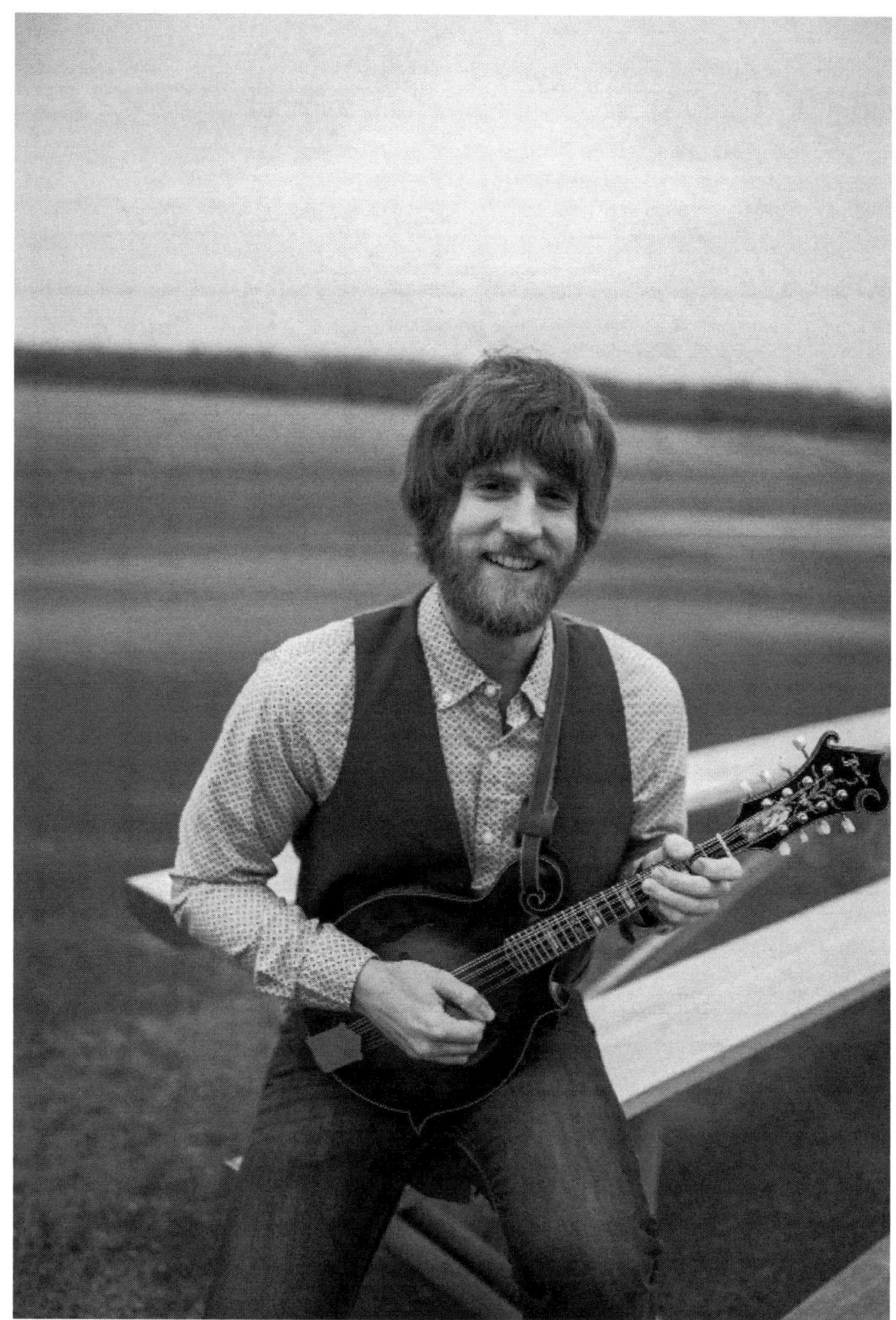

Tommy Norris

Tommy Norris is a 2010 graduate of Western Carolina University where he studied classical music, jazz and music theory, along with a focus in music technology. Since then, he has employed his mandolin talents as a teacher and composer. As a member and co-founder of "The Barefoot Movement", Tommy continually tours nationally, bringing their brand of acoustic music to new audiences. When not on tour, he resides in Raleigh, North Carolina spending his time teaching, composing, and recording.

Other Mel Bay Mandolin Books

100 Tunes from O'Neill's Music of Ireland for Mandolin (Allison)
Celtic Mandolin (Driscoll)
Celtic Mandolin Encyclopedia (Bancalari)
Fiddle Tunes & Irish Music for Mandolin (Gelo)
Irish Music for Mandolin Made Easy (Berthoud)
Irish Mandolin Playing: A Complete Guide (Berthoud)
Steve Kaufman's Favorite Celtic Reels for Mandolin
Steve Kaufman's Favorite 50 Celtic Reels A-L for Mandolin
Steve Kaufman's Favorite 50 Celtic Jigs and Waltzes for Mandolin
Steve Kaufman's Favorite Celtic Hornpipes for Mandolin
Tunes from 17th-Century Scotland Arranged for Mandolin (MacKillop)
Turlough O'Carolan for Mandolin (Landau)
Anthology of Mandolin Music (Orr)
International Favorites for Mandolin (Carr)
Italian Folk Music for Mandolin (LaBarbera)
Mandolin Sampler (Gelo)
Mandolin Songbook (Eidson)
Mandolin Tunes Made Easy: Large Print (W. Bay)
Mandolin Uff Da! Let's Dance: Scandinavian Fiddle Tunes & House Party Music (Bruce)
Master Anthology of Mandolin Solos Vol. 1 (Multiple Authors)
Northern Italian & Ticino Region Folk Songs for Mandolin (Aonzo/Ponzoni/Borsani)
Traditional Southern Italian Mandolin and Fiddle Music (LaBarbera)
World Music for Mandolin Made Easy (Berthoud)
50 Tunes for Mandolin Vol. 1 (Geslison)
101 Red Hot Bluegrass Mandolin Licks & Solos (McCabe)
A Smoky Mountain Christmas for Mandolin (Kaufman)
All-Time Favorite Parking Lot Picker's Mandolin Solos (Bruce)
Backup Trax/Old-Time & Fiddle Tunes for Fiddle and Mandolin (Bruce)
Blazing Mandolin Solos (Kaufman)
Bluegrass Breaks: Mandolin (Bruce)
Chris Thile: Stealing Second
Classic Bluegrass Solos for Mandolin (Collins)
Complete Jethro Burns Mandolin (Burns/Eidson)
Doc and Dawg (Grisman and Watson)
Favorite Mandolin Picking Tunes (Bruce)
Great Mandolin Picking Tunes (Carr)
Kenny Hall's Music Book: Old-Time Music for Fiddle & Mandolin (Hall/Gray)
Lively Mandolin Tunes (Norris)
Mandolin Gospel Tunes (Carr)
Mandolin Picking Tunes - An Early American Christmas (Norris)
Monroe Instrumentals: 25 Bill Monroe Favorites (Collins)
New Classics for Bluegrass Mandolin (Baldassari)

Other Mel Bay Mandolin Books

Old-Time Mandolin Solos (Eidson/Hayth)
Old-Time Stringband Workshop for Mandolin (Keefer/Weissman/Prohaska)
Old-Time Favorites for Fiddle and Mandolin (Levenson)
Old-Time Festival Tunes for Fiddle and Mandolin (Levenson)
Parking Lot Picker's Play-Along: Mandolin (Bruce)
Parking Lot Picker's Songbook (Bruce)
Shady Grove (Grisman)
Southern Mountain Mandolin (Erbsen)
Steve Kaufman's Favorite 50 Mandolin Tunes A-F
Steve Kaufman's Favorite 50 Mandolin Tunes G-M
Steve Kaufman's Favorite 50 Mandolin Tunes N-S
Steve Kaufmans Favorite 50 Mandolin Tunes S-W
String Band Classics for Mandolin (Bruce)
Texas Fiddle Favorites for Mandolin (Carr)
The Mike Marshall Collection
Tone Poems for Mandolin (Grisman)
12 Divertimentos for Solo Mandolin (Oswald/Goodin)
18th Century Mandolin Duets of Jean-Baptiste Miroglio (ed. Barry Trott)
Airs for the Seasons Arranged for Solo Mandolin (Oswald/Goodin)
Bach E Major Prelude from the Partita No. 3 for Solo Violin Transcribed for Mandolin
(Driscoll) Bach's Sonatas and Partitas for Solo Violin Arranged for Mandolin (Driscoll)
Baroque Music for Mandolin (Bancalari)
Baroque Sampler for Octave Mandolin (Goodin)
Cantabile (Baldassari/Mock)
French Baroque Mandolin Suite (Marais/Bancalari)
German Baroque Music for Mandolin (Bancalari)
J. S. Bach for Mandolin (Bancalari)
J. S. Bach Mandolin Duets (Holenko)
J. S. Bach: Two-Part Inventions for Two Mandolins (Bancalari)
Mandolin Classics (Cherednik/Eidson)
Mandolin Classics in Tablature (Bancalari)
Mandolin Instrumentals (Landau)
Mandolin Picking Tunes - Early Music Gems (Bruce)
Playford for Mandolin (Goodin)
Renaissance Solos for Mandolin (Holenko)
Romantic Melodies for Mandolin Solo (Landau)
Telemann for Mandolin (Goodin)
Telemann for Two Mandolins (Goodin)
Tunes from 17th-Century Scotland Arranged for Mandolin (MacKillop)
Vivaldi Concertos for Mandolin (Lemma)
Wedding Music for Mandolin (Bruce)
Wohlfahrt Violin Studies Arranged for Mandolin (Case)

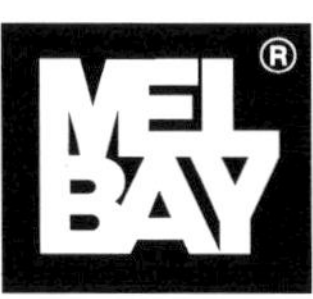